REMAIN IN A CAR.
IT IS SAFER
THAN THE
OPEN
DO
DO GET UNDER
A CLIFF OR LEDGE
DO GO INDOORS
IF POSSIBLE
LIE DOWN IN DITCH
OR HOLLOW IF STORM
IS SEVERE AND NO
OTHER SHELTER IS
AROUND
D1292525

LIGHTNING AND THUNDER

by **HERBERT S. ZIM**

Illustrated by
James Gordon Irving

WILLIAM MORROW & COMPANY
New York 1952

Thanks are due to Paul Lehr,
Air Force Weather School, Chanute Air Force Base,
Rantoul, Illinois,
for reading and criticising the manuscript.

Printed in the United States of America.

Published simultaneously in the Dominion of Canada by George J. McLeod Limited, Toronto
Library of Congress Catalog Card Number: 52-5063

At any moment, day or night, about eighteen hundred thunderstorms crash and flash the world over. All these storms, big and little, add up to about a hundred flashes of lightning a second, day in and day out. There are always thunderstorms somewhere, though you may see only a dozen or two a year.

AVERAGE NUMBER OF THUNDERSTORMS EACH YEAR

Along the California coast perhaps only one or two thunderstorms a year are seen, but on the west coast of Florida ninety to a hundred days a year are darkened by thunderclouds. Thunderstorms are more common during summer, and they are more common during the afternoon than at any other time of day. Thunderstorms

over the ocean are likely to form soon after mid-night, in the early hours of the morning. The reasons for all this go back to one beginning—the beginning of lightning and thunder.

Lightning and thunder seem very different from fog, clouds, rain, wind, heat, and other things which make up the weather. Yet without knowing about the rest of the weather, one cannot understand lightning and thunder. Long ago, before scientists had begun to study the

weather, everyone was afraid of lightning and thunder. To the ancient Greeks and Romans, thunder was the angry voice of their great god Zeus, or Jupiter.

The Norsemen believed the flashes and crashes that made wrongdoers tremble occurred when Thor swung his mighty hammer. Today we

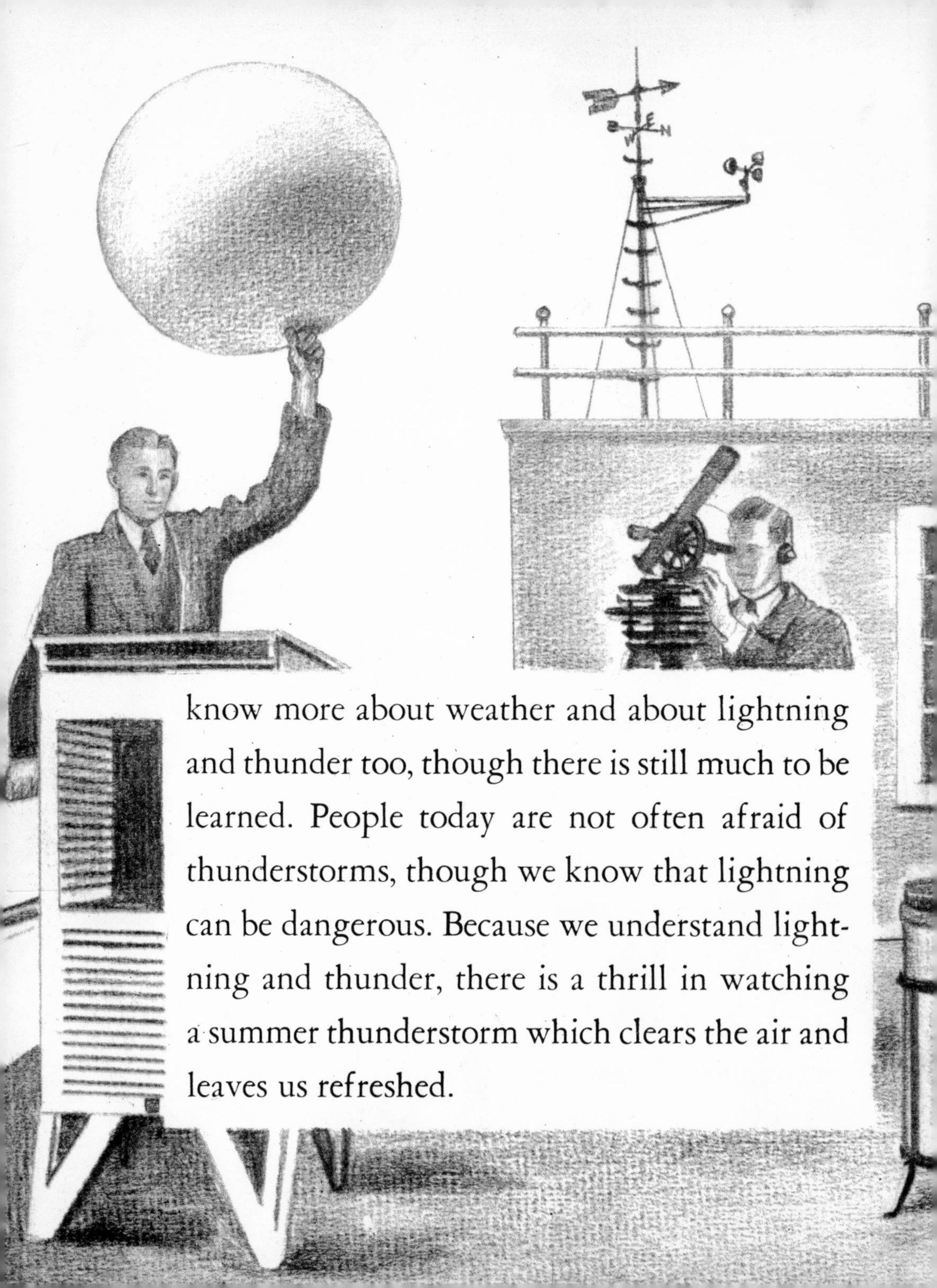

know more about weather and about lightning and thunder too, though there is still much to be learned. People today are not often afraid of thunderstorms, though we know that lightning can be dangerous. Because we understand lightning and thunder, there is a thrill in watching a summer thunderstorm which clears the air and leaves us refreshed.

Place a piece of dark metal and a piece of light-colored wood or cloth of about the same size side by side in the sunlight on a bright afternoon. Touch them after a while, or set a thermometer on each. You will find the dark metal is hotter, though both have been warmed by the sun for

DARK METAL AND WHITE CLOTH
IN FULL SUNLIGHT

the same length of time. This is because some things absorb more heat from the sun than others, depending on their color, form, and material. A plowed field of black soil becomes

HOW THE SUN HEATS DIFFERENT SOILS

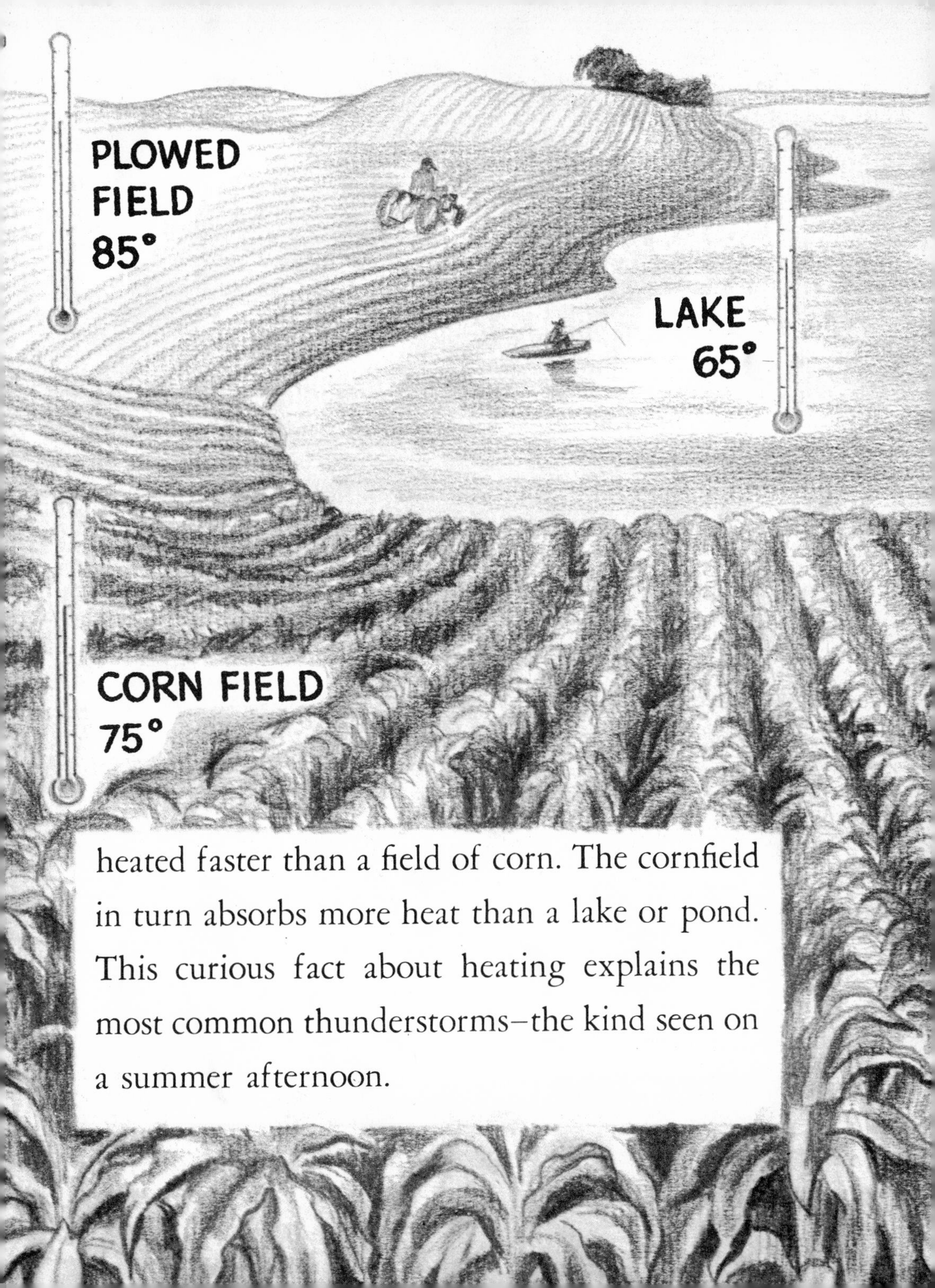

heated faster than a field of corn. The cornfield in turn absorbs more heat than a lake or pond. This curious fact about heating explains the most common thunderstorms–the kind seen on a summer afternoon.

On a summer day some parts of the land absorb more heat than others. By late morning these places are definitely warmer than the land around them. As the land is warmed, it warms the air lying upon it. And, since most things become slightly larger as they are heated, this warmed air begins to expand and so occupies

more space. Because of expansion, any container of warm air weighs less than another container the same size full of cold air. Imagine a great block of air a mile wide, a mile long, and a mile

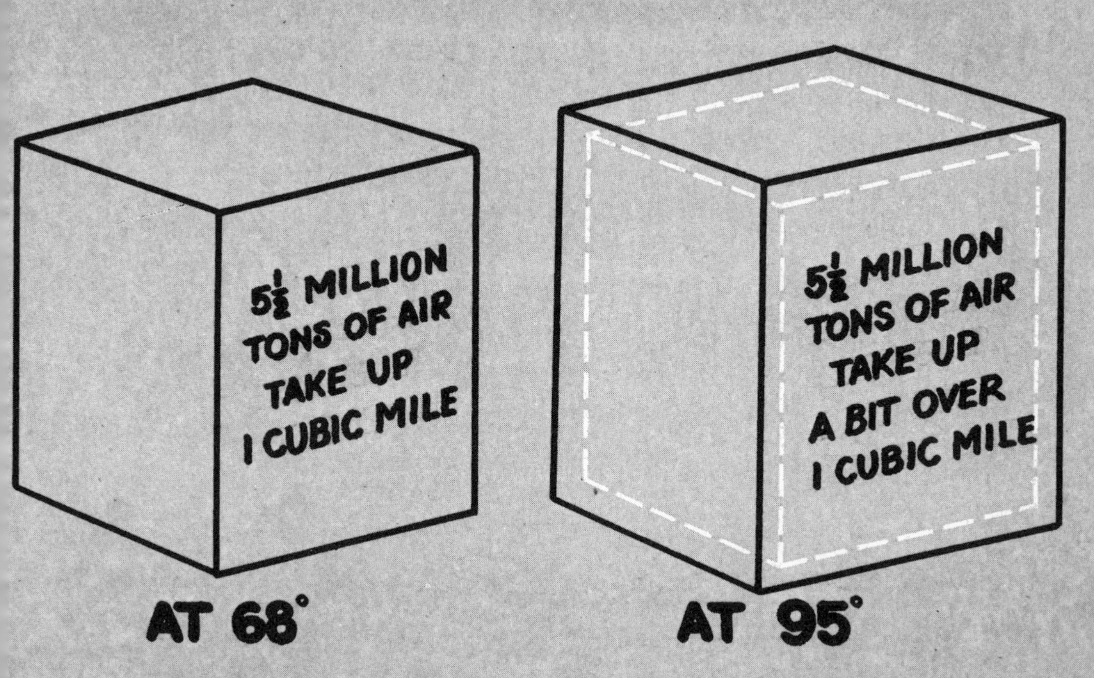

ANY WEIGHT OF AIR
TAKES UP MORE ROOM WHEN IT IS HEATED

high (one cubic mile). On a summer morning when the temperature is 68 degrees, this great block of air weighs a little over five and a half million tons. On a hot afternoon when the temperature has gone up to 95 degrees and the air has expanded, the cubic mile of air weighs about five and a quarter million tons, or over a quarter of a million tons less.

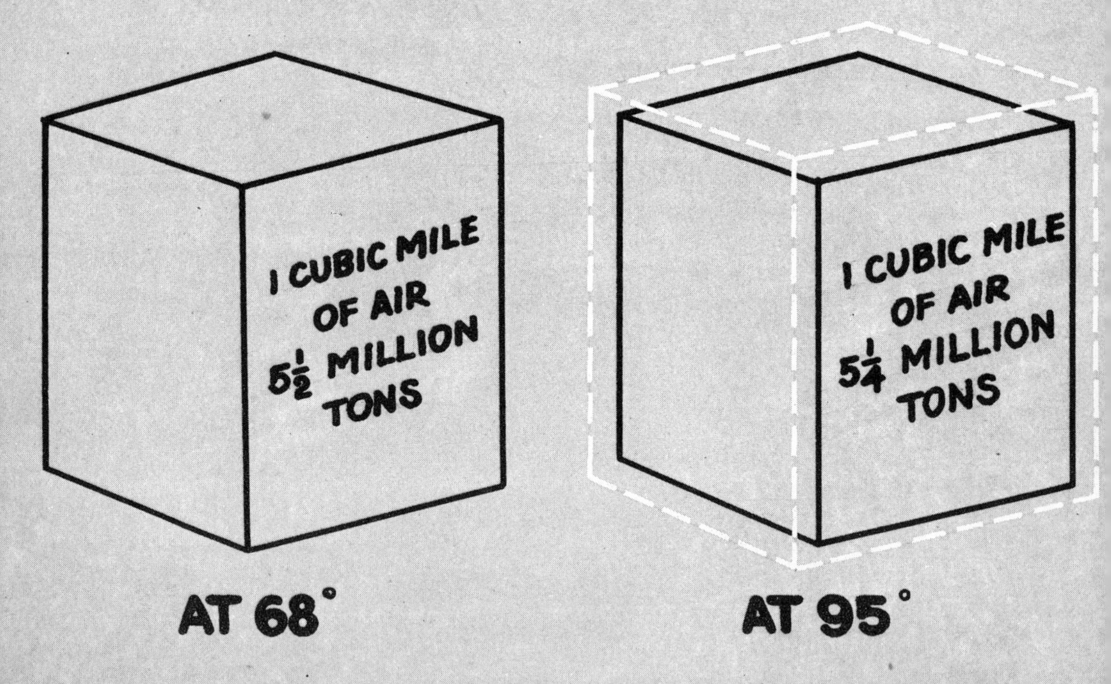

AS THE TEMPERATURE INCREASES, A CUBIC MILE OF AIR EXPANDS — AND SO HAS A LOSS OF WEIGHT

As air warms and becomes lighter than the air around it, it begins to rise like an invisible balloon. Before it stops, when it has cooled to the same temperature as the surrounding air, the warmed air has risen three, four, or five miles. Rising air cools because the higher you go, the

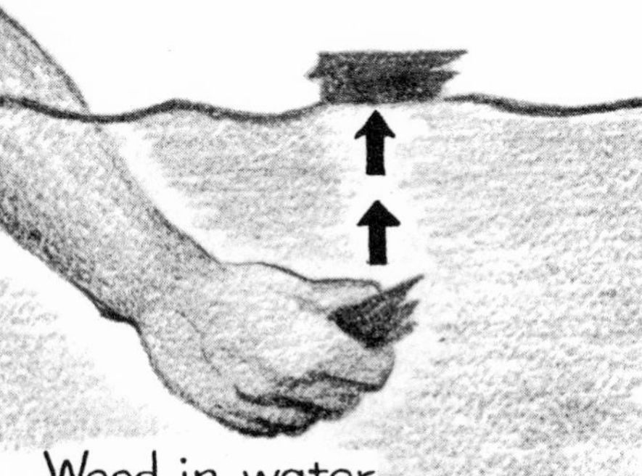
Wood in water

Iron in mercury

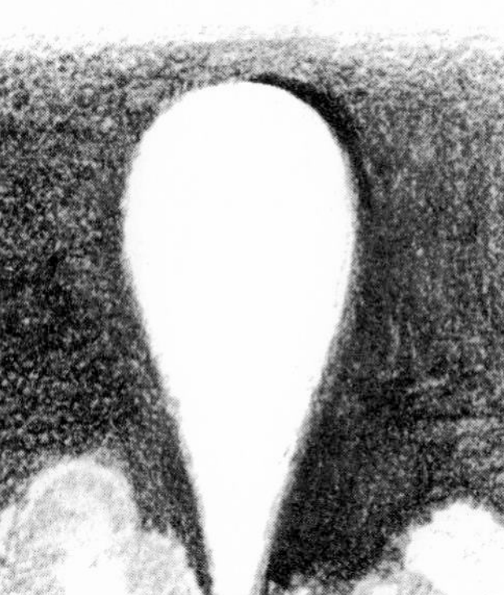
A helium balloon in the air

Warm air in cold air

LIGHTER THINGS RISE

colder it gets. One mile up, a thermometer reads about seventeen degrees cooler than on the ground; two miles up about thirty-four degrees cooler. It is from eighty-five to over a hundred degrees colder at five miles up—always well below freezing, even on the hottest days. At this level, water in the air often takes the form of tiny ice crystals.

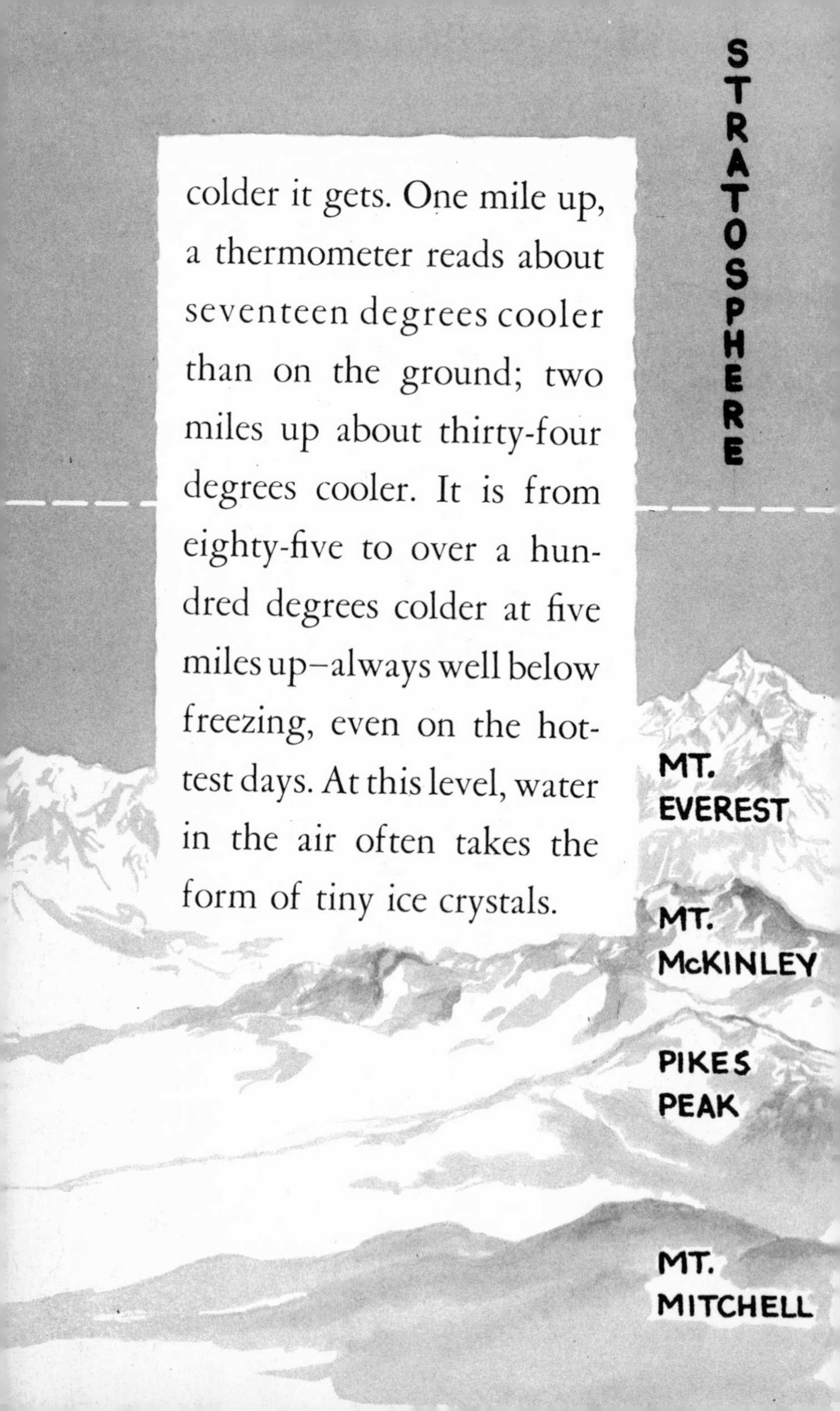

STRATOSPHERE

MT. EVEREST

MT. McKINLEY

PIKES PEAK

MT. MITCHELL

Rising warm air creates something like an ir
visible chimney as it rises. Other air moves i
from all sides, making an upward current or up
draft. As air rises in the updraft and cools, it ca
hold less and less moisture. All air contains som
moisture or water vapor, especially during sun

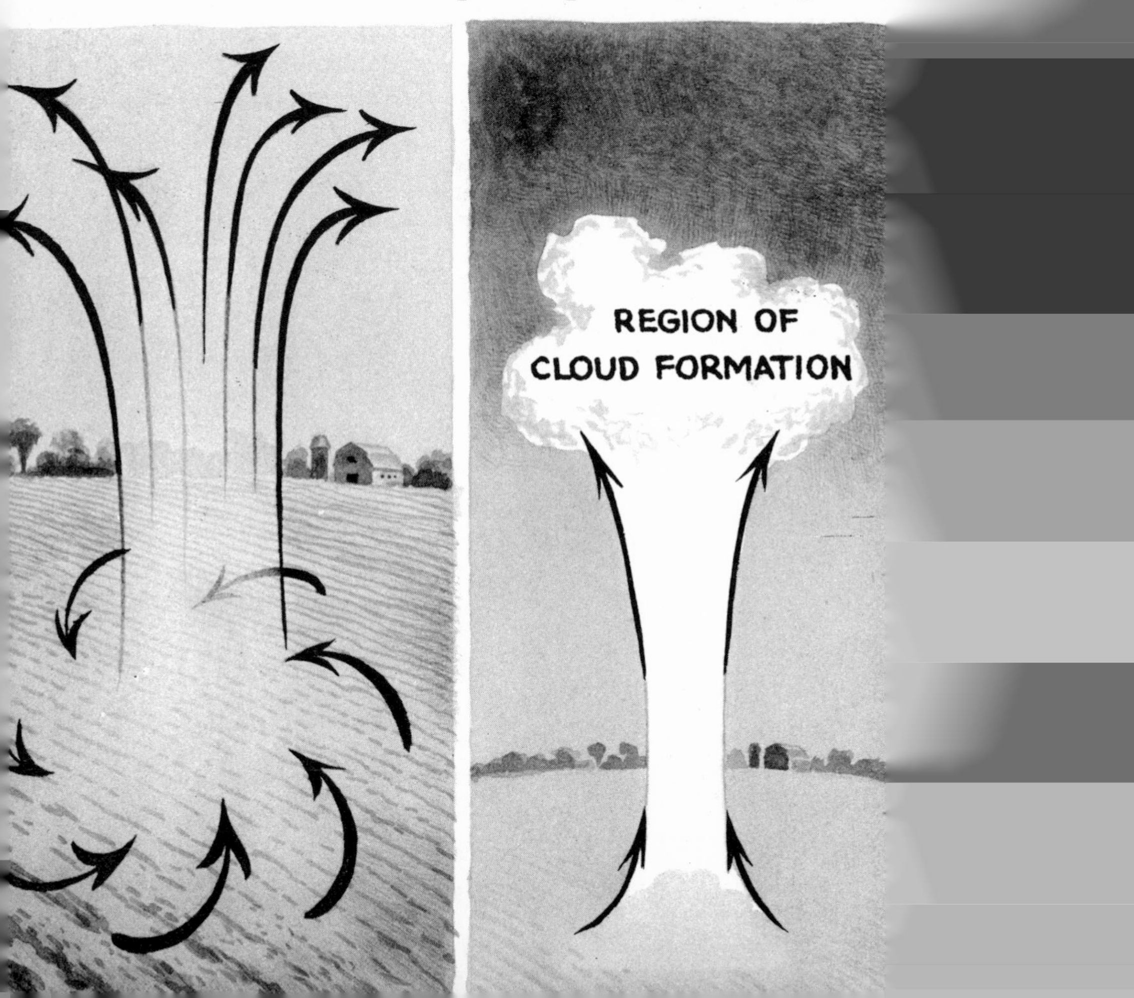

mer in our part of the world. As air rises a mile, or two, or three, and cools, some of the water vapor condenses to form tiny droplets of water, droplets so small that some two hundred million of them would scarcely make a teaspoonful of water. Most of the clouds you see are made of these droplets.

WARM AIR,
IN CONTACT
WITH A
CHILLED
SURFACE,
IS COOLED,
LOSES ITS
MOISTURE,
AND DEPOSITS
IT ON GLASS AND PITCHEF

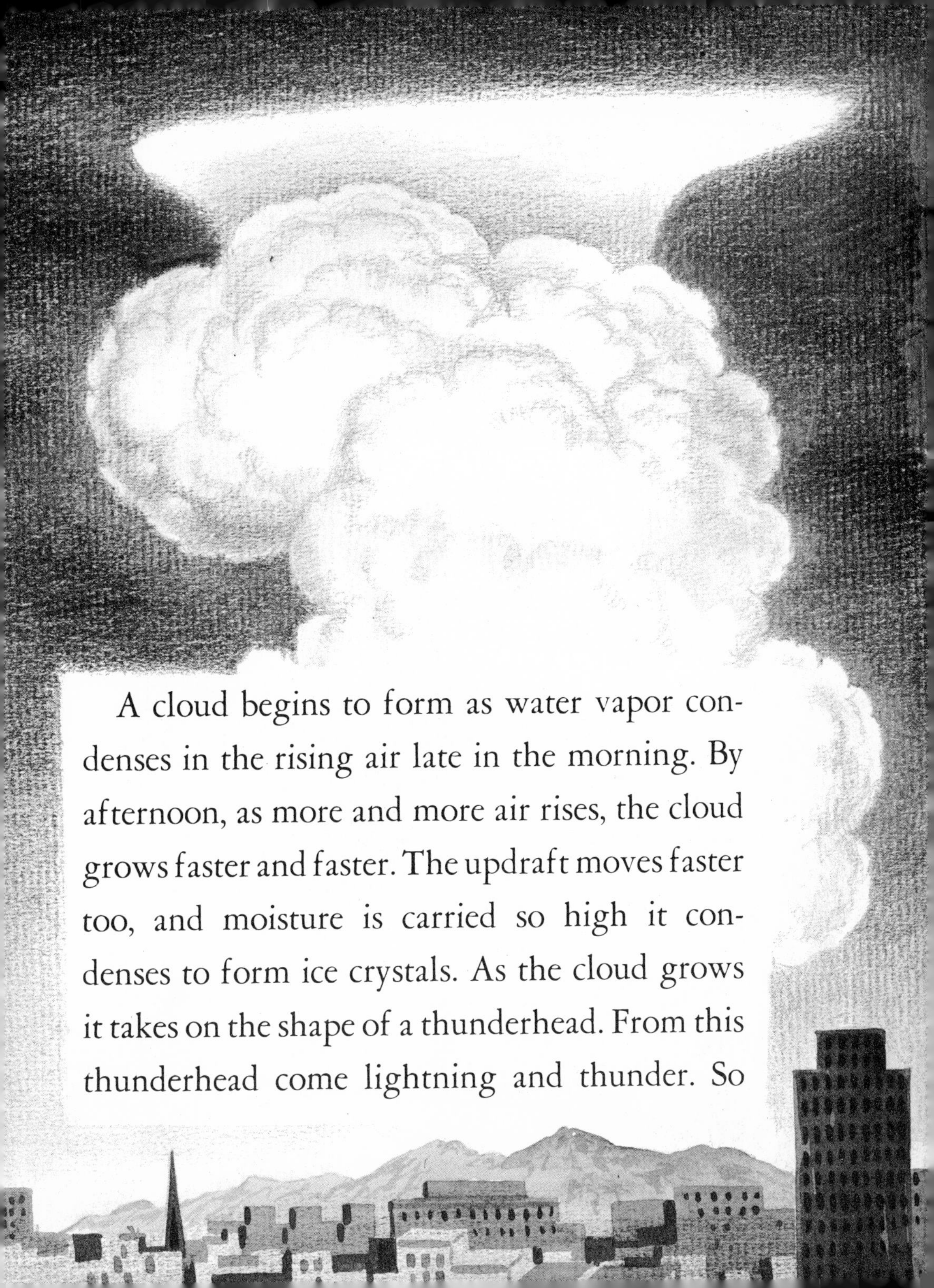

A cloud begins to form as water vapor condenses in the rising air late in the morning. By afternoon, as more and more air rises, the cloud grows faster and faster. The updraft moves faster too, and moisture is carried so high it condenses to form ice crystals. As the cloud grows it takes on the shape of a thunderhead. From this thunderhead come lightning and thunder. So the unequal heating of the earth and the rising columns of warmed air cause much of our lightning and thunder. Because there is more of this heating in summer than in winter, and because the heating has increased by afternoon, there are more thunderstorms on summer afternoons than at any other time. These facts are clear, but *how* lightning and thunder are born in the thunderhead is something we do not yet fully understand.

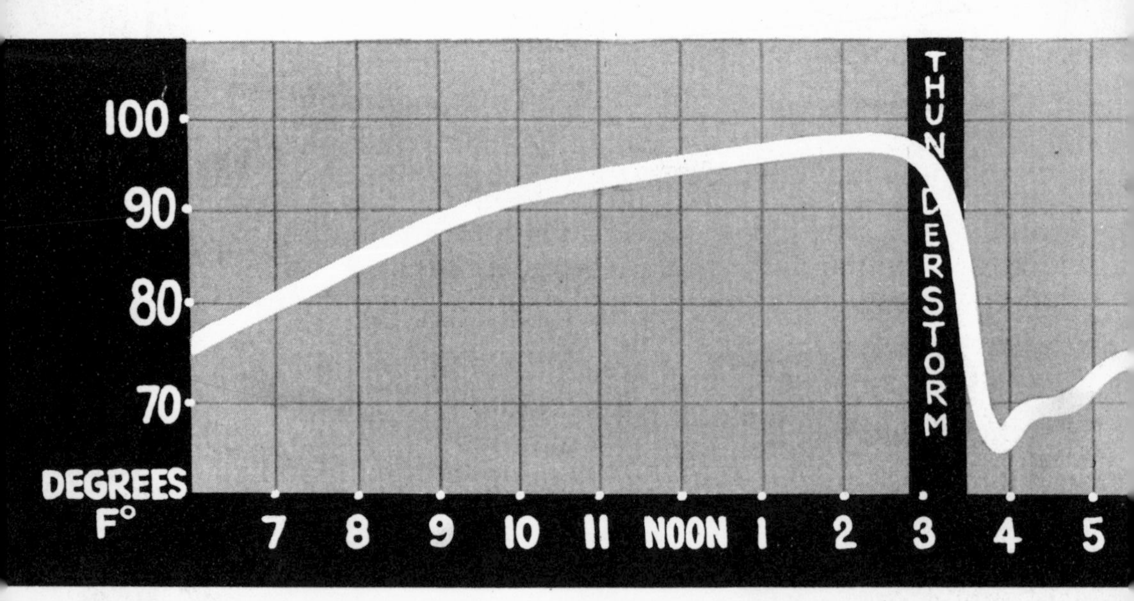

TEMPERATURE ON A THUNDERSTORM DAY
(AFTER W. J. HUMPHREYS)

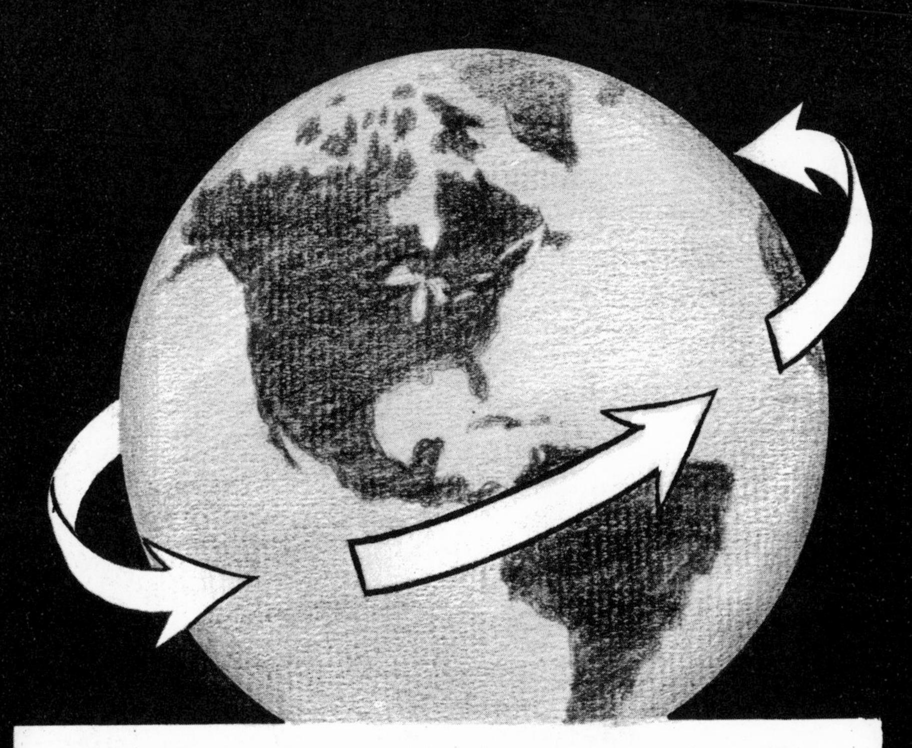

Possibly because it is spinning around, and for other reasons too, the earth generates an electrical charge–a negative electrical charge. The air, a very poor conductor of electricity, has an electrical charge also, but its charge is much too weak to cause lightning. The updraft in a thunderhead creates new electrical charges and increases the charges in the air a thousand times more than normal.

EXPERIMENTS WITI

(THESE WORK BES

PRODUCE NEGATIVE CHARGES BY RUBBING HARD RUBBER, SEALING WAX, AND SOME PLASTICS WITH WOOL OR FUR

UNLIKE CHARGES (+ AND
LIKE CHARGES (+ AND + C

PRODUCE POSITIVE CHARGES BY RUBBING GLASS WITH SILK

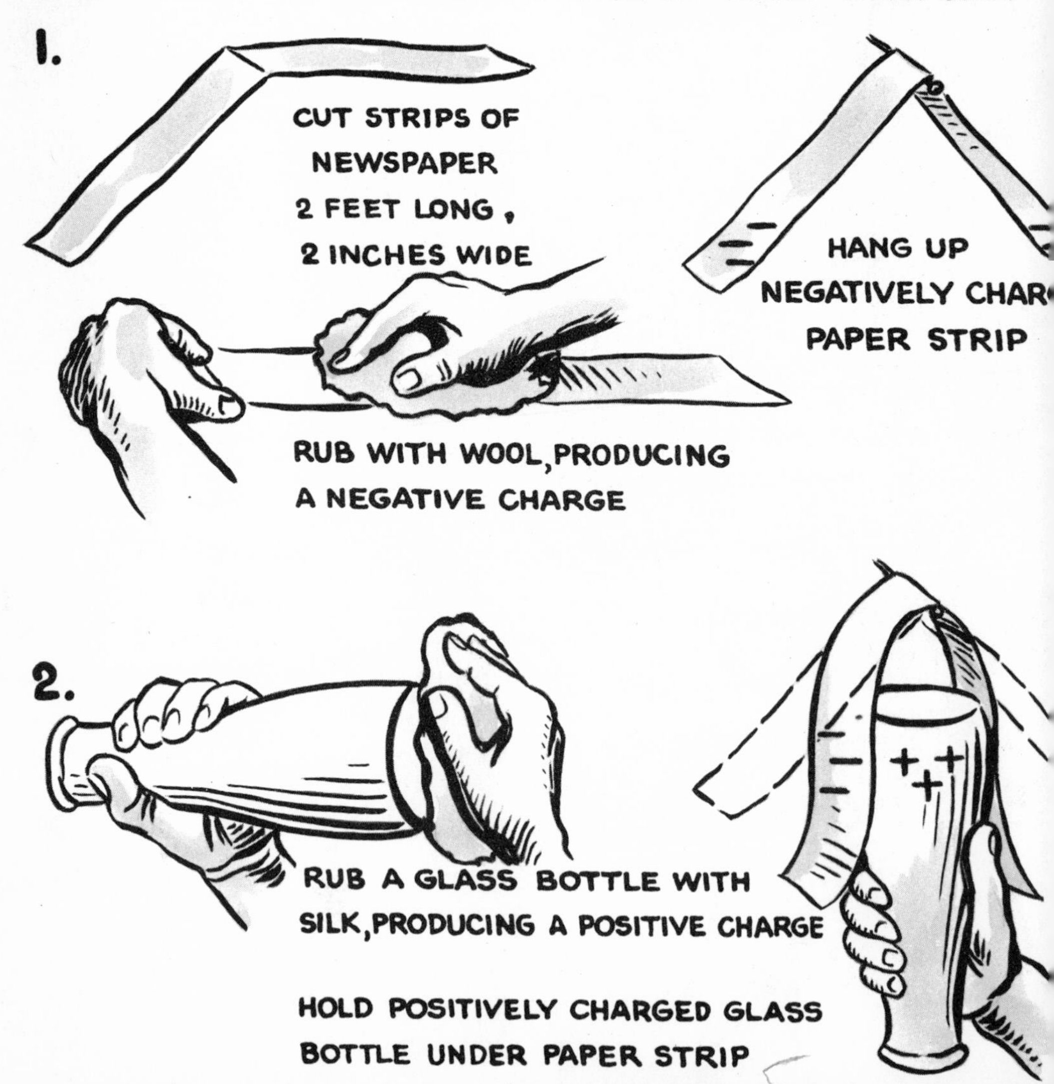

1.
CUT STRIPS OF NEWSPAPER 2 FEET LONG, 2 INCHES WIDE
HANG UP NEGATIVELY CHAR
PAPER STRIP
RUB WITH WOOL, PRODUCING A NEGATIVE CHARGE
2.
RUB A GLASS BOTTLE WITH SILK, PRODUCING A POSITIVE CHARGE
HOLD POSITIVELY CHARGED GLASS BOTTLE UNDER PAPER STRIP

LECTRICAL CHARGES

N COLD DRY DAYS)

R – AND +) ATTRACT

AND –) REPEL OR PUSH AWAY

HOLD NEGATIVELY CHARGED COMB UNDER PAPER STRIP

3.

RUB BACK OF COMB WITH WOOL, PRODUCING A NEGATIVE CHARGE

4.

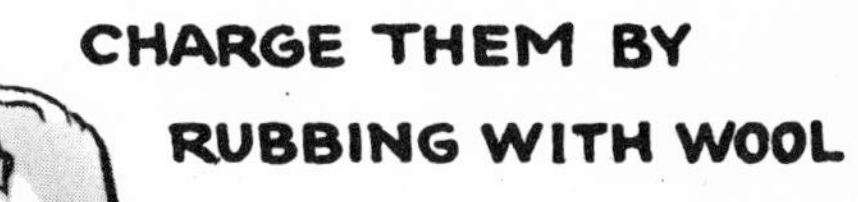

CHARGE THEM BY RUBBING WITH WOOL

UNCHARGED BALLOONS HANG TOGETHER

CHARGED BALLOONS REPEL EACH OTHER

5.

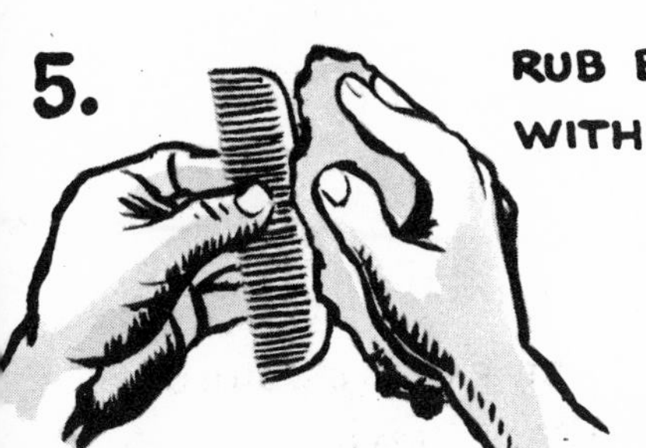

RUB BACK OF COMB WITH WOOL

HOLD NEAR FAUCET AND ATTRACT A TRICKLE OF WATER

As the updraft in the thunderhead pushes higher and faster, water droplets join together to form rain. This rain and the gusty winds mark the start of a thunderstorm. Some of the rain falls to the ground. But in thunderstorms over the dry Western plains the rain may evaporate before it reaches the earth, and the thunderstorm is a dry one. However, because of the strong up-

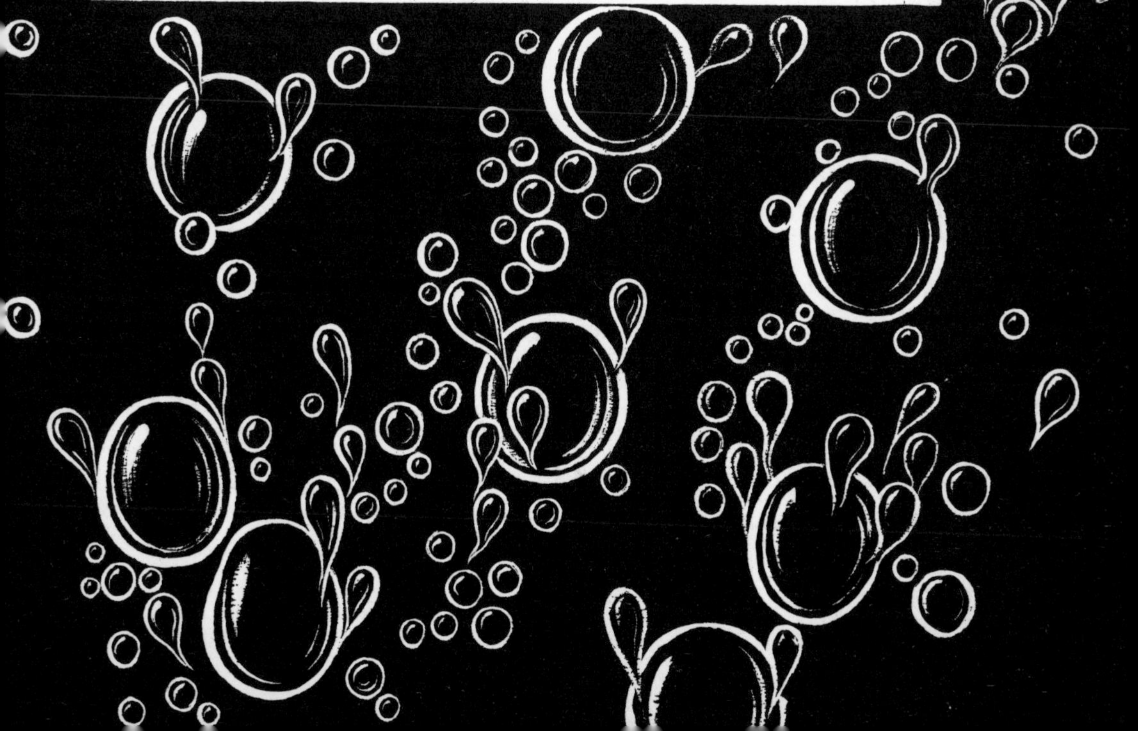

RAINDROPS TORN APART IN AN UPDRAFT

SMALLER, NEGATIVE PARTICLES ASCENDING

LARGE, POSITIVE PARTICLES FALLING

draft in every thunderstorm, some of the rain goes *up* instead of down. Rain cannot fall through air which is moving upward faster than 17 miles per hour. When the updraft is faster, it tears the raindrops apart and carries the smaller droplets up with it. As raindrops are torn apart, the larger droplets become charged with positive electricity. The smaller droplets which are carried aloft pick up negative electrical charges. The ice crystals high in the cloud have posi-

tive charges. Soon the thunderhead is strongly charged with different charges in different parts of the cloud. These strong positive and negative charges are the immediate cause of lightning.

The electrical charges in thunderheads are not the same as an electric current. The charges only become a current when they move, as from one part of the cloud to another or from the cloud to the earth. Electricity does not flow easily through air as it does through copper, iron, or silver. Metals do not resist the flow of electricity and so are good conductors. Wood, paper, and air have high resistance and so are poor conductors, or insulators. As the charges in a thunder-

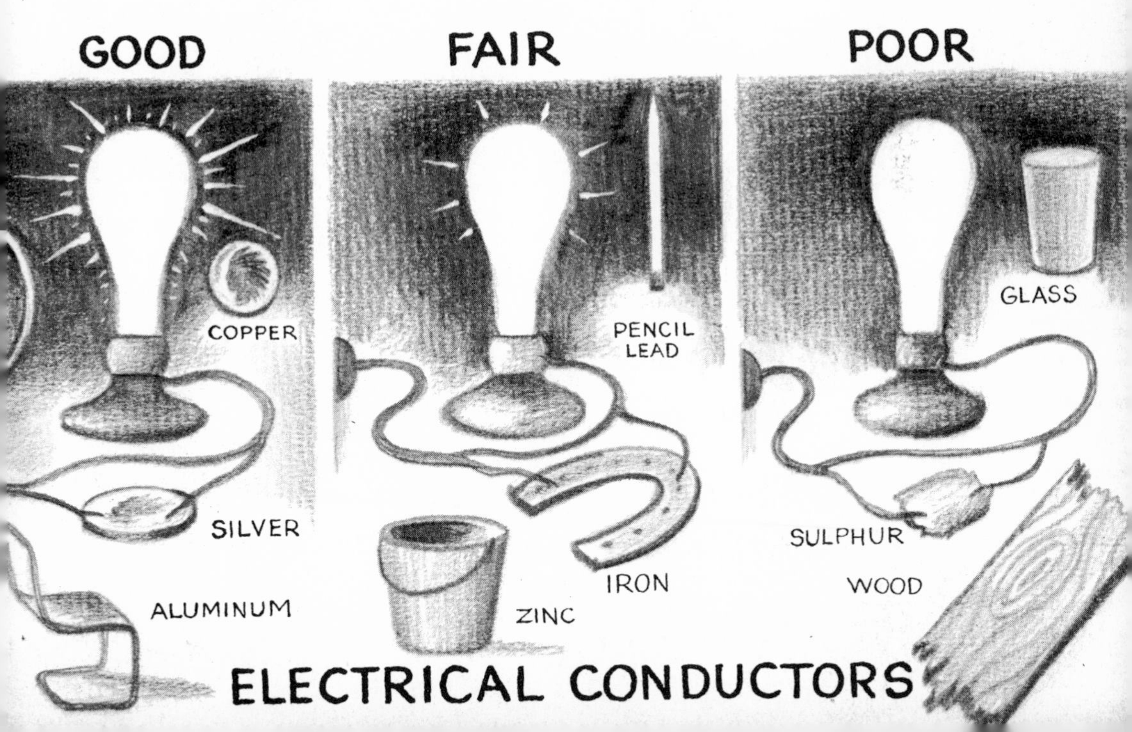

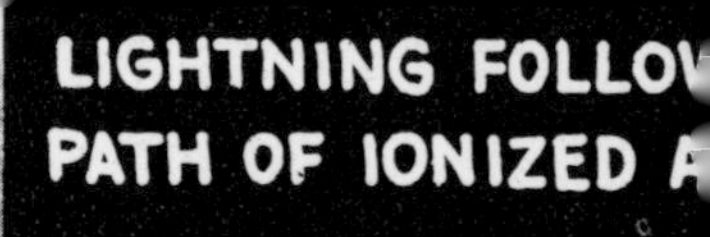

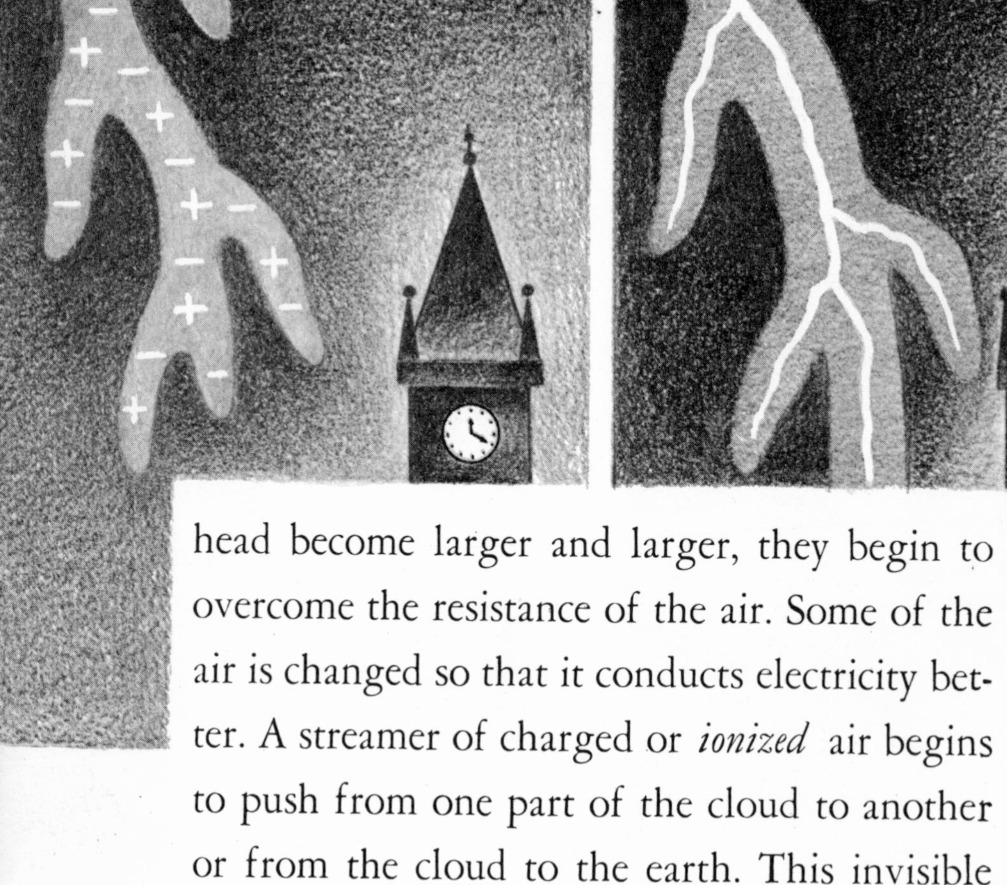

head become larger and larger, they begin to overcome the resistance of the air. Some of the air is changed so that it conducts electricity better. A streamer of charged or *ionized* air begins to push from one part of the cloud to another or from the cloud to the earth. This invisible charged streamer is a much better conductor of electricity than the rest of the air, and the elec-

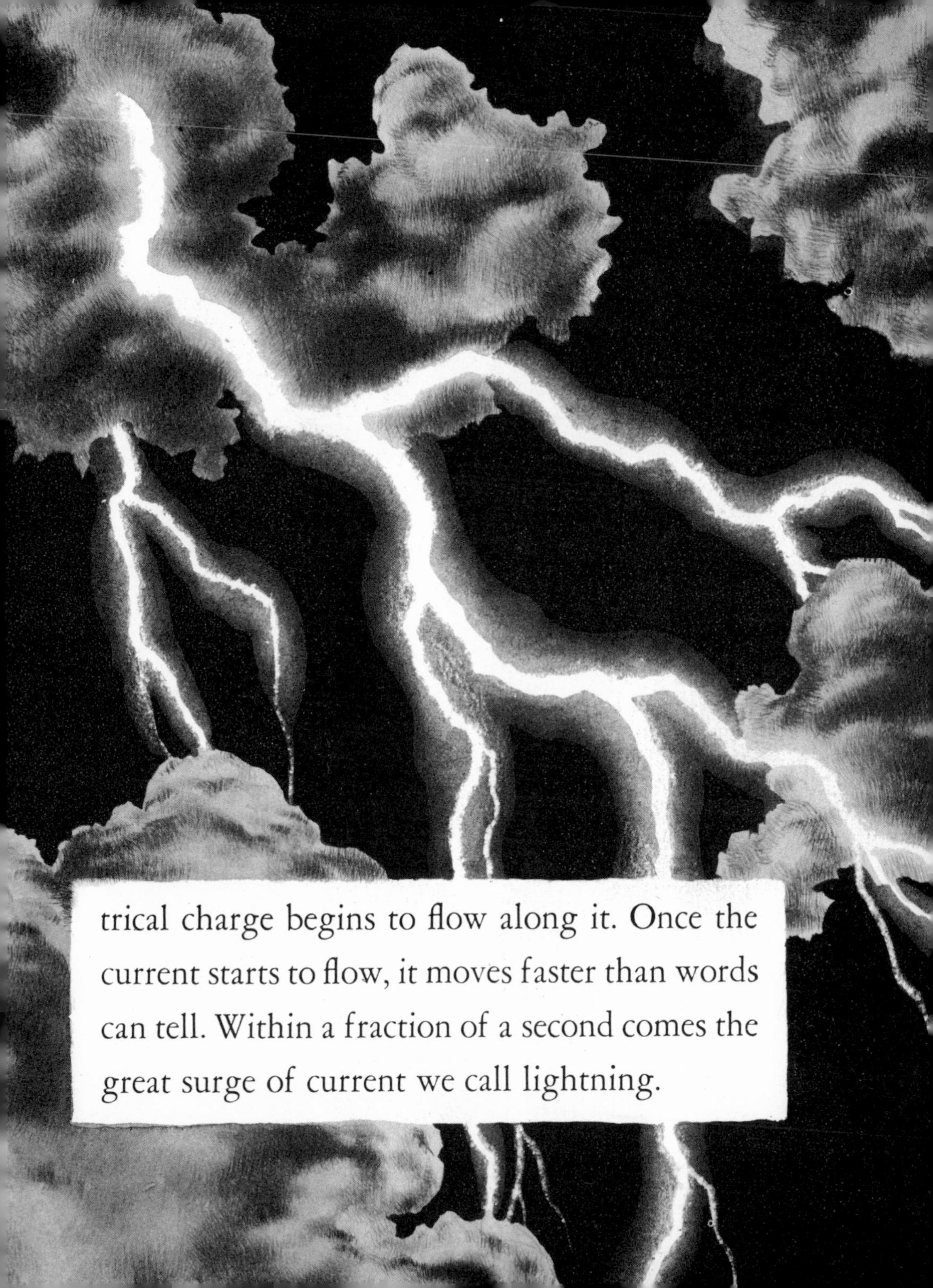

trical charge begins to flow along it. Once the current starts to flow, it moves faster than words can tell. Within a fraction of a second comes the great surge of current we call lightning.

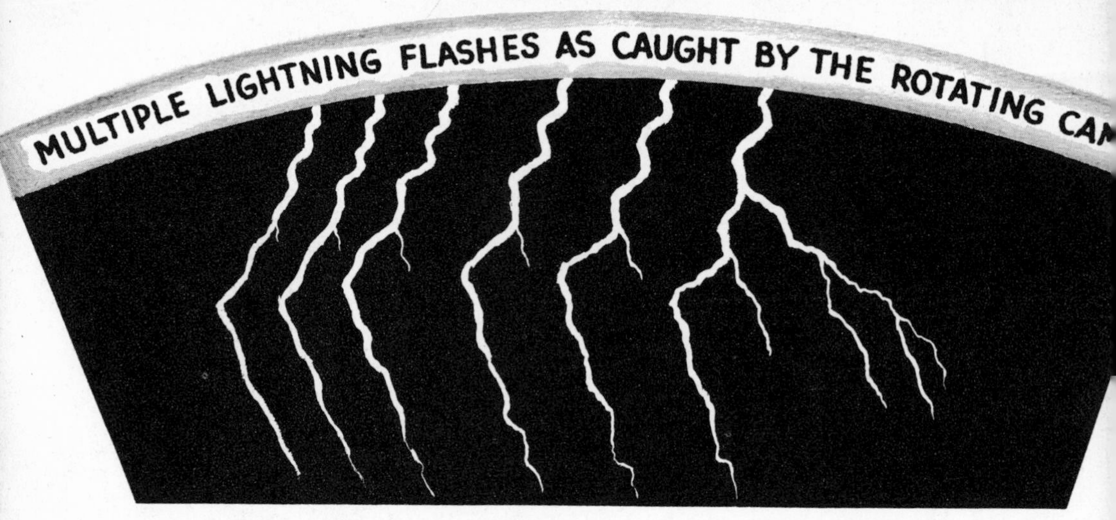

A flash of lightning takes less than one ten-thousandth of a second. It seems to last longer because it is so bright. Moreover, what seems to be a single flash of lightning may be a dozen or more flashes in about the same path. Photographs of lightning taken with a fast-moving camera prove that many rapid strokes often fol-

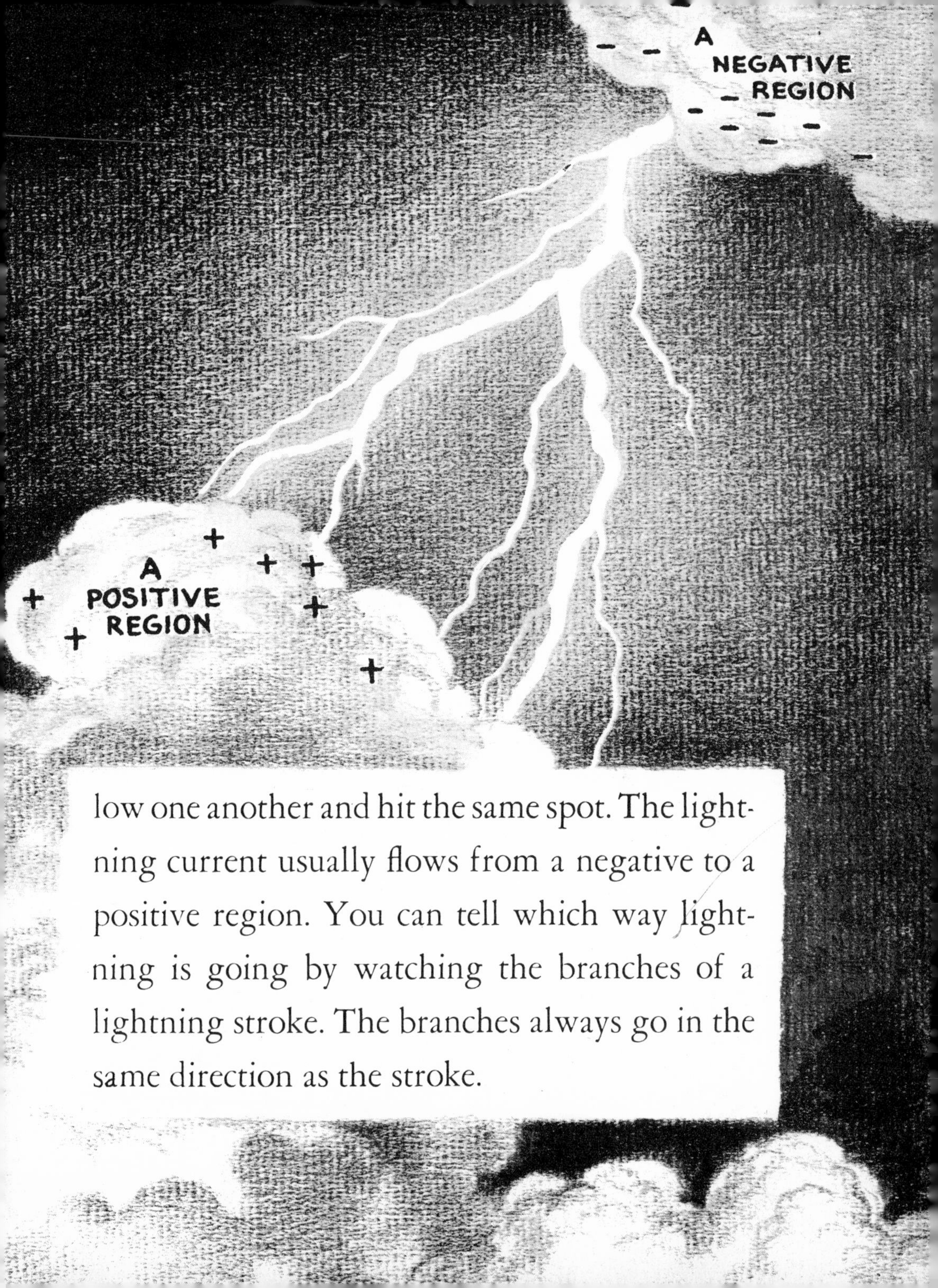

low one another and hit the same spot. The lightning current usually flows from a negative to a positive region. You can tell which way lightning is going by watching the branches of a lightning stroke. The branches always go in the same direction as the stroke.

A lightning flash which is from several inches to a foot wide and from 500 feet to over 2 miles long, comes from a tremendous electric current, so powerful that it has never been duplicated in a laboratory. The current we use in a two-battery flashlight has a push or voltage of about 3 volts; an automobile battery has 6 volts; the current used in most of our homes pushes with 110 or

TWO-BATTERY FLASHLIGHT 3 VOLTS

110 VOLTS

ELECTRIC LIGHT BULB

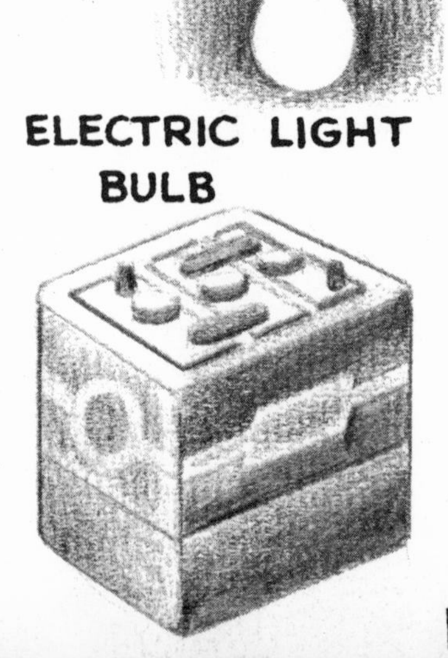

AUTOMOBILE BATTERY - 6 VOLTS

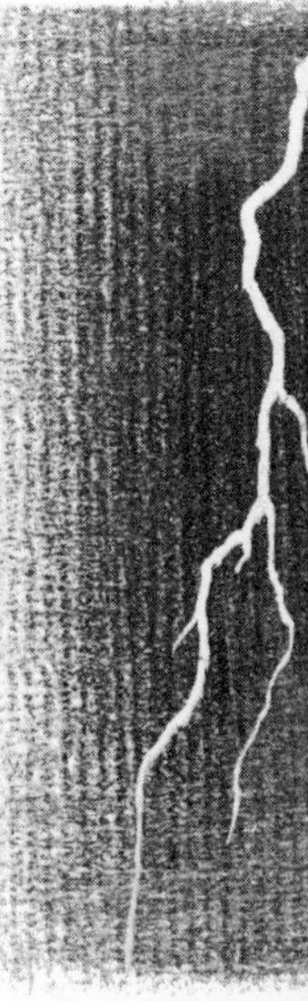

UP TO ONE BILL VOLTS

VOLT X AMPERES = WATTS WATTS ÷ VOLTS

115 volts. The voltage of lightning is at least many millions, and is often a billion volts or more. The amount of current that flows through a medium-sized electric light bulb is about one ampere. A small fan takes about 5 amperes. An electric iron or toaster takes about 10 amperes. A lightning flash runs as high as a hundred thousand amperes, or even more.

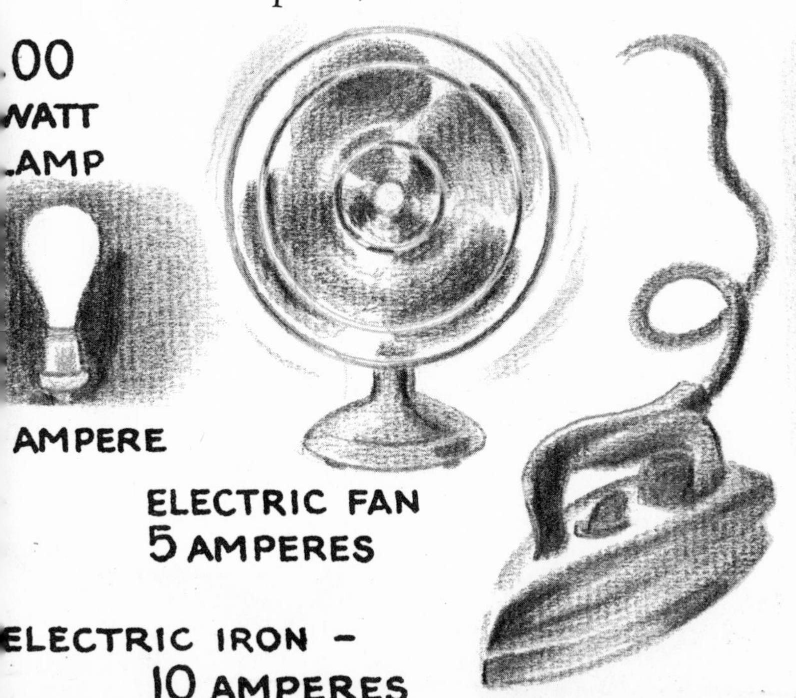

It seems strange that we have never found a way to use the strongest electric current in the world. Yet the reason is clear—the current flows for only a very brief part of a single second. Schemes to get electricity from lightning do not work, because we cannot control such a great, yet brief, current. There is no way to change lightning into current suitable for daily use. If such a change were possible, a single large thunderstorm would yield about forty thousand dollars' worth of electricity. Engineers see so many difficulties in attempting to harness and use lightning that no serious efforts are being made to do it. Instead, engineers try to improve the electric supply we now get from huge dams and steam generating plants.

Though lightning is the same the world over, it sometimes appears in different forms. These depend largely on the position of the observer. Common lightning with straight or branching strokes is called chain or streak lightning. Forks and a jagged pattern seem more common in the first of a close series of flashes, before a good path of charged air is formed.

Sheet lightning is lightning seen far away, or when the flash is hidden from direct view, and is only seen as it is reflected from clouds. This blurred lightning is best seen at night. On rare occasions a lightning flash leaves a line of bright beads or spots behind when it fades. This beaded lightning is chain lightning. It is in such a position that one sees an end view of branch strokes, which look brighter and seem to last longer because of the way they are seen.

SHEET
LIGHTNING
BEADED
LIGHTNING
TYPES OF

CHAIN OR
STREAK
LIGHTNING
GHTNING

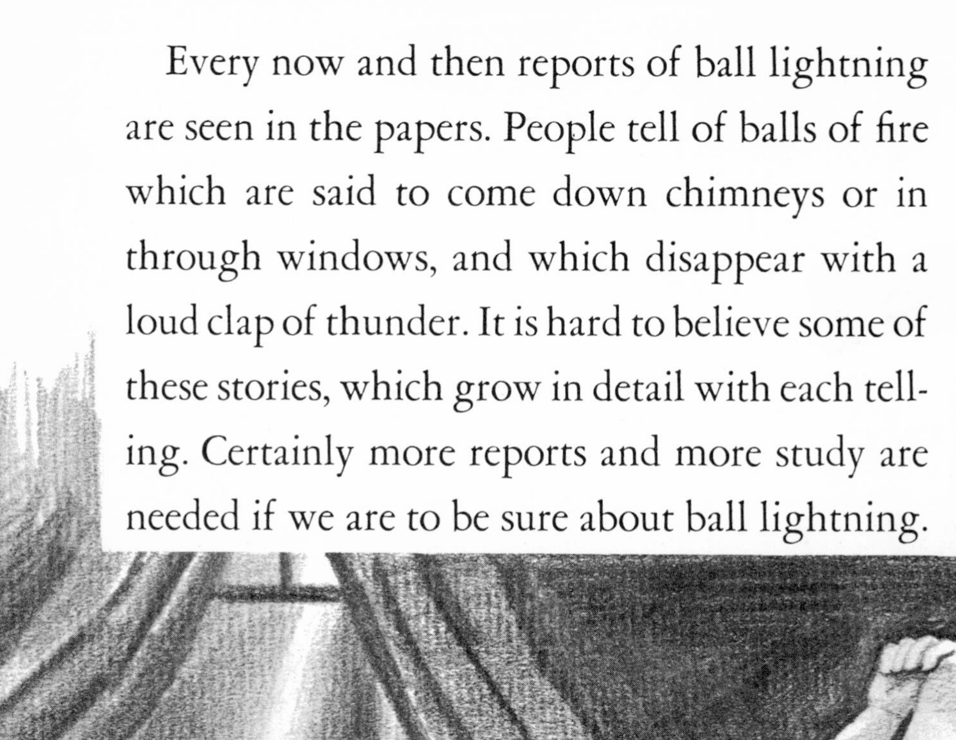

Every now and then reports of ball lightning are seen in the papers. People tell of balls of fire which are said to come down chimneys or in through windows, and which disappear with a loud clap of thunder. It is hard to believe some of these stories, which grow in detail with each telling. Certainly more reports and more study are needed if we are to be sure about ball lightning.

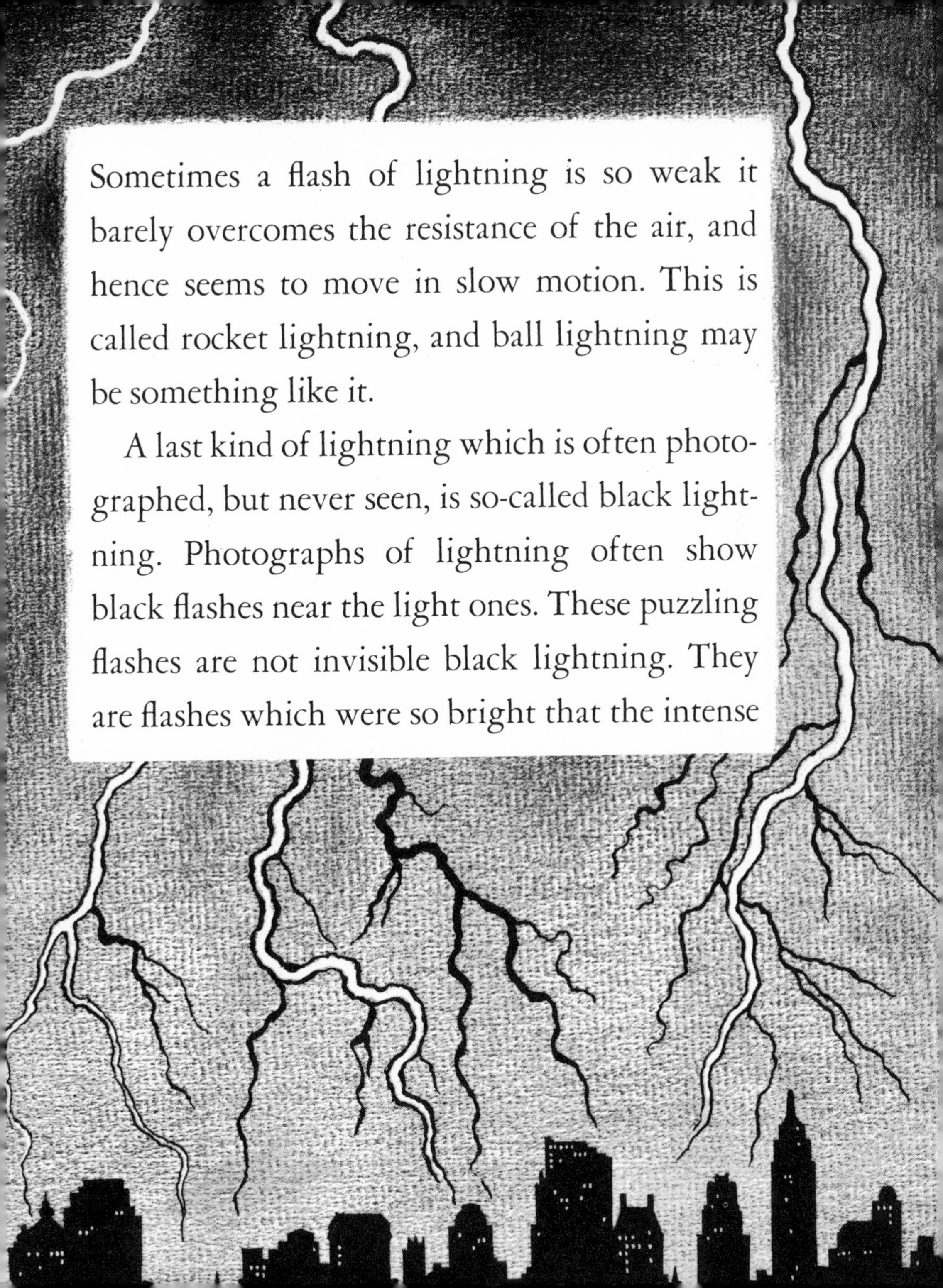

Sometimes a flash of lightning is so weak it barely overcomes the resistance of the air, and hence seems to move in slow motion. This is called rocket lightning, and ball lightning may be something like it.

A last kind of lightning which is often photographed, but never seen, is so-called black lightning. Photographs of lightning often show black flashes near the light ones. These puzzling flashes are not invisible black lightning. They are flashes which were so bright that the intense

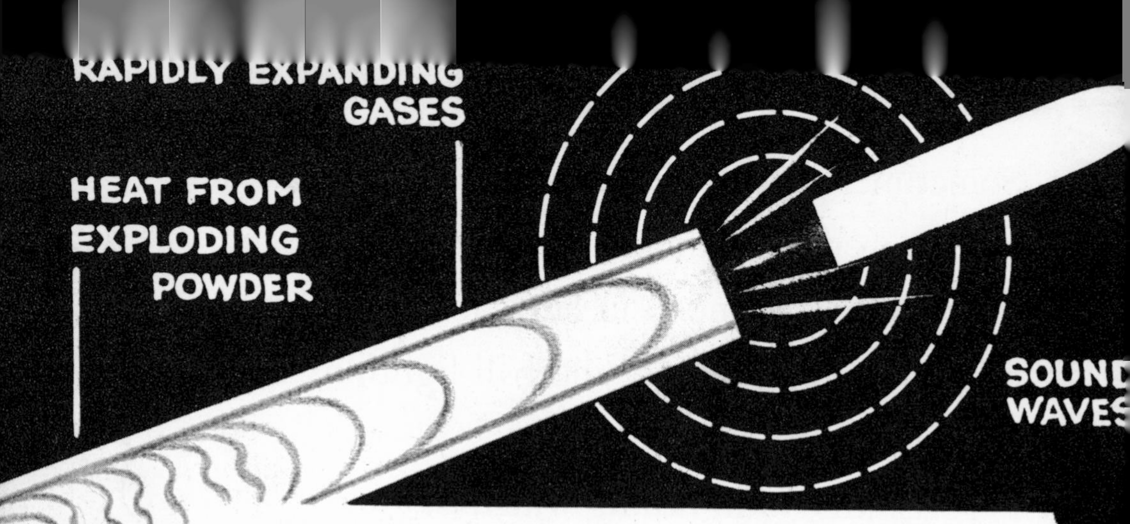

light destroyed the sensitive chemicals in the film. This produces the black streak in the photograph which often bewilders people who do not know how it is caused.

No matter what its form, the effects of lightning are often strange and sometimes dangerous. Of these, thunder is the best known. Now and then you may hear a roll of thunder without seeing a lightning flash. You may be sure there was a flash, perhaps a distant or hidden one, because the sound of thunder is always caused by lightning.

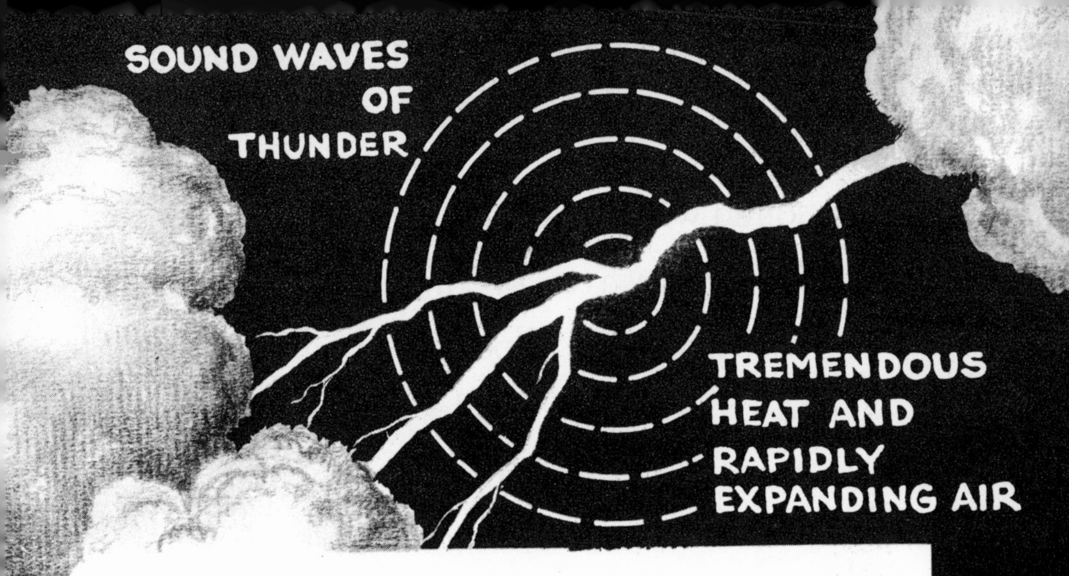

It is well agreed that the great heat of the lightning flash causes thunder, which, in some ways, is like the roar of a cannon. The heat and expanding gases from exploding powder cause the sound or compression waves that make the cannon's roar. The temperature of a lightning flash is much higher than that of exploding powder. It is believed to be something like the temperature on the surface of the sun. This heat is so great that compression and shock waves are thrust out in all directions, making the crash and rumble we hear.

The sound waves of thunder are very different from the light waves of the lightning flash. Sound waves travel at a speed of about 1100 feet a second or about 750 miles per hour. Light waves travel at the enormous speed of 186,000 miles a *second*—about a million times faster than sound. No wonder the flash of lightning is seen before the thunder is heard.

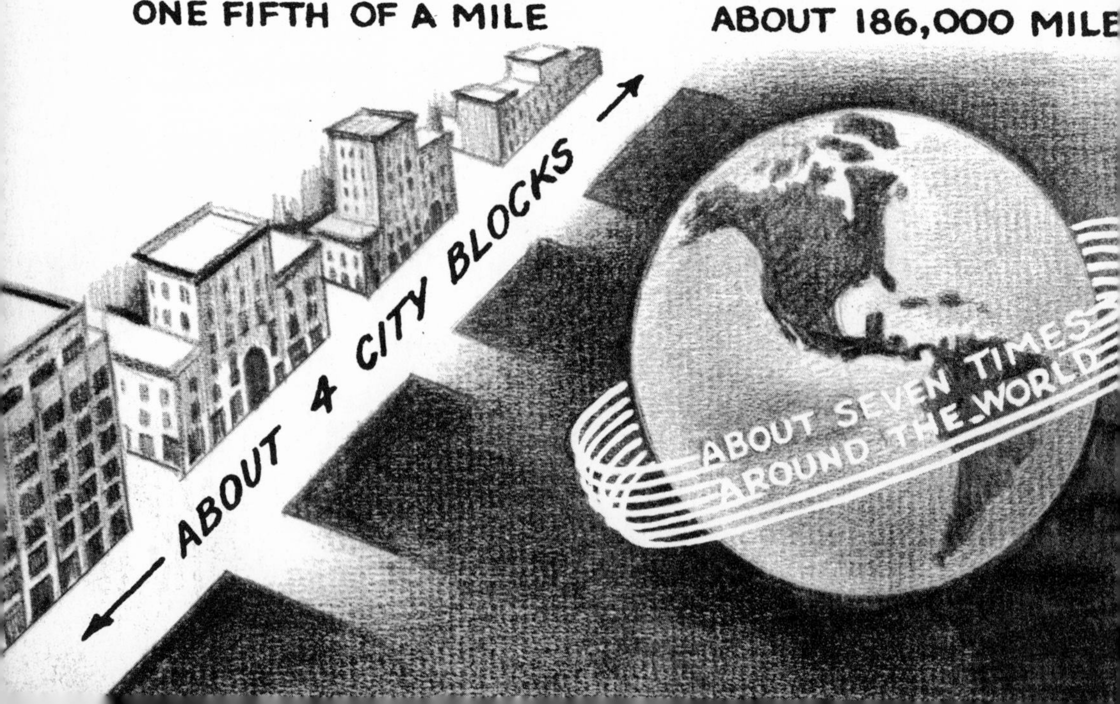
IN ONE SECOND
SOUND TRAVELS ABOUT
ONE FIFTH OF A MILE
LIGHT TRAVELS
ABOUT 186,000 MILE
ABOUT 4 CITY BLOCKS
ABOUT SEVEN TIMES
AROUND THE WORLD

You can easily tell your distance from a lightning flash because of the difference between the speed of light and the speed of sound. Counting the number of seconds between the flash and the thunder will give you the answer. If you lack a watch, tell the seconds by counting slowly: a thousand and one, a thousand and two, etc. This slow counting gives you the seconds; the chart shows you how far away the flash was.

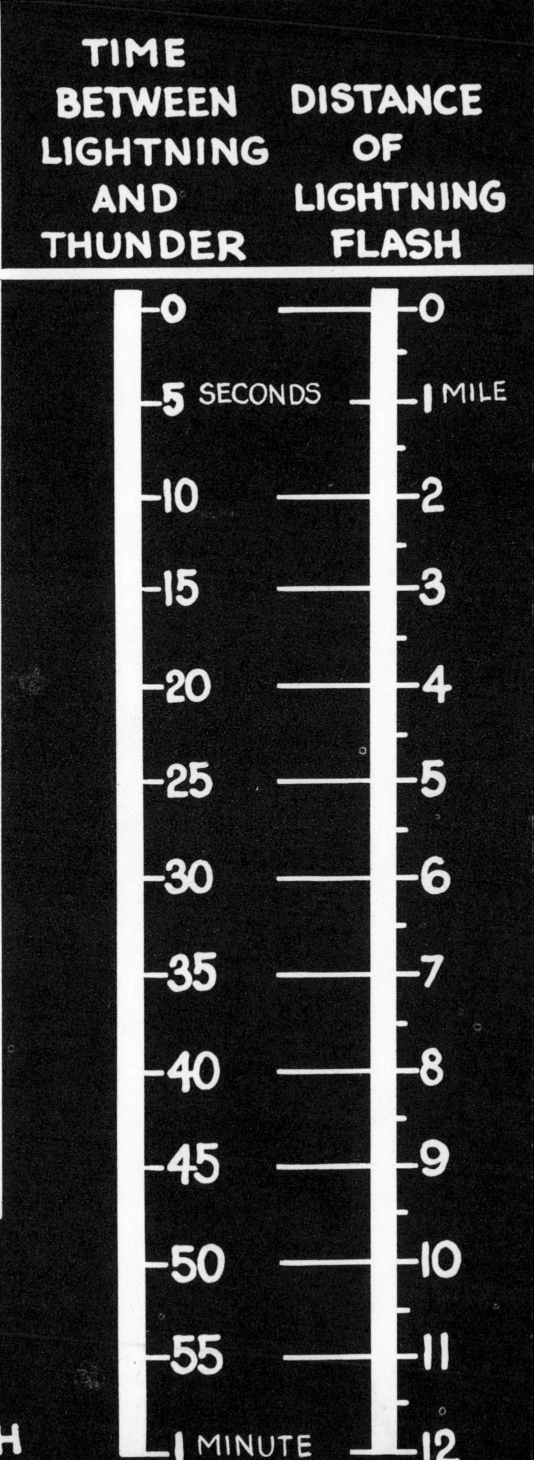

TIME BETWEEN LIGHTNING AND THUNDER	DISTANCE OF LIGHTNING FLASH
0	0
5 SECONDS	1 MILE
10	2
15	3
20	4
25	5
30	6
35	7
40	8
45	9
50	10
55	11
1 MINUTE	12

CHART

TO TELL YOUR DISTANCE FROM A LIGHTNING FLASH

When a thunderstorm is near, the thunder is loud and sharp. Ordinarily thunder cannot be heard more than ten or fifteen miles away, and then it is a low rumble instead of a clear-cut report. The rumble of thunder may also be due to echoes. It is also caused, in part, by the long, sometimes crooked path of lightning. Thunder does not all start at the same place and so does

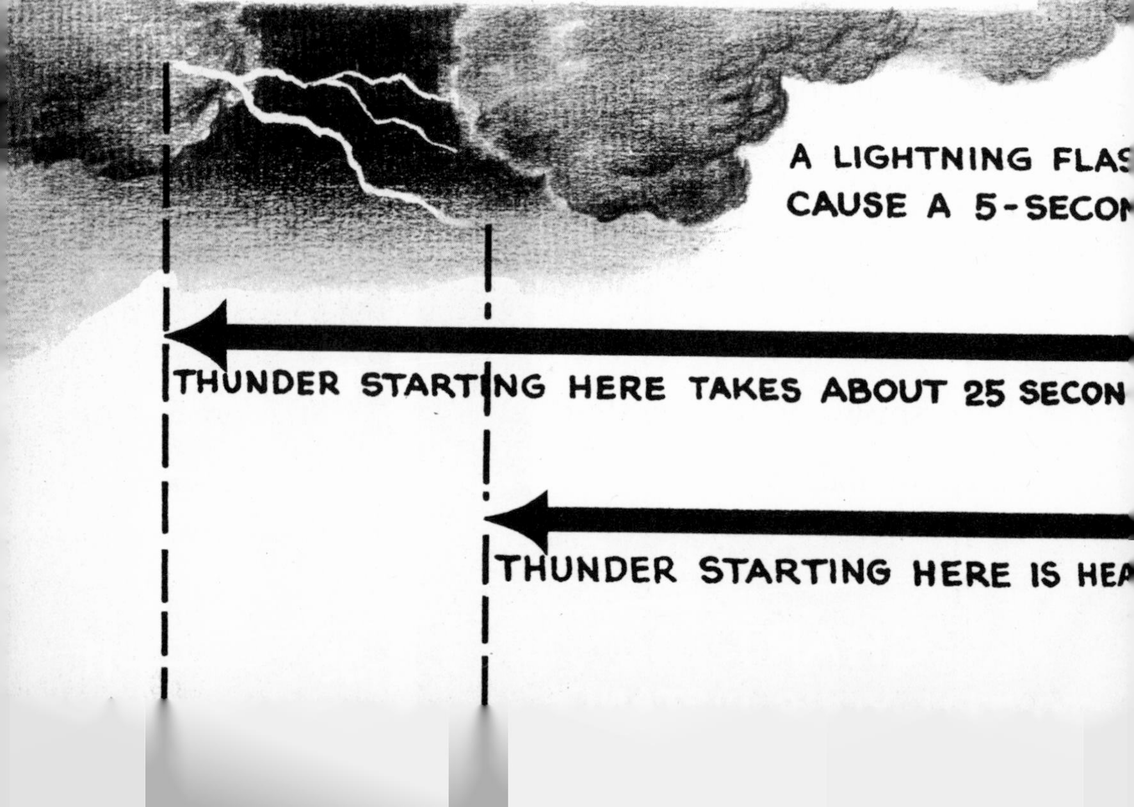

A LIGHTNING FLAS
CAUSE A 5-SECON

THUNDER STARTING HERE TAKES ABOUT 25 SECON

THUNDER STARTING HERE IS HEA

not all reach your ear at the same time. While lightning may be dangerous, thunder never is. By the time you hear the roar or the rumble, the lightning flash is over.

Besides causing thunder, the heat of lightning has other effects. When lightning strikes a tree with a ripping crash, the heat produced by the current flowing through the wet wood turns the

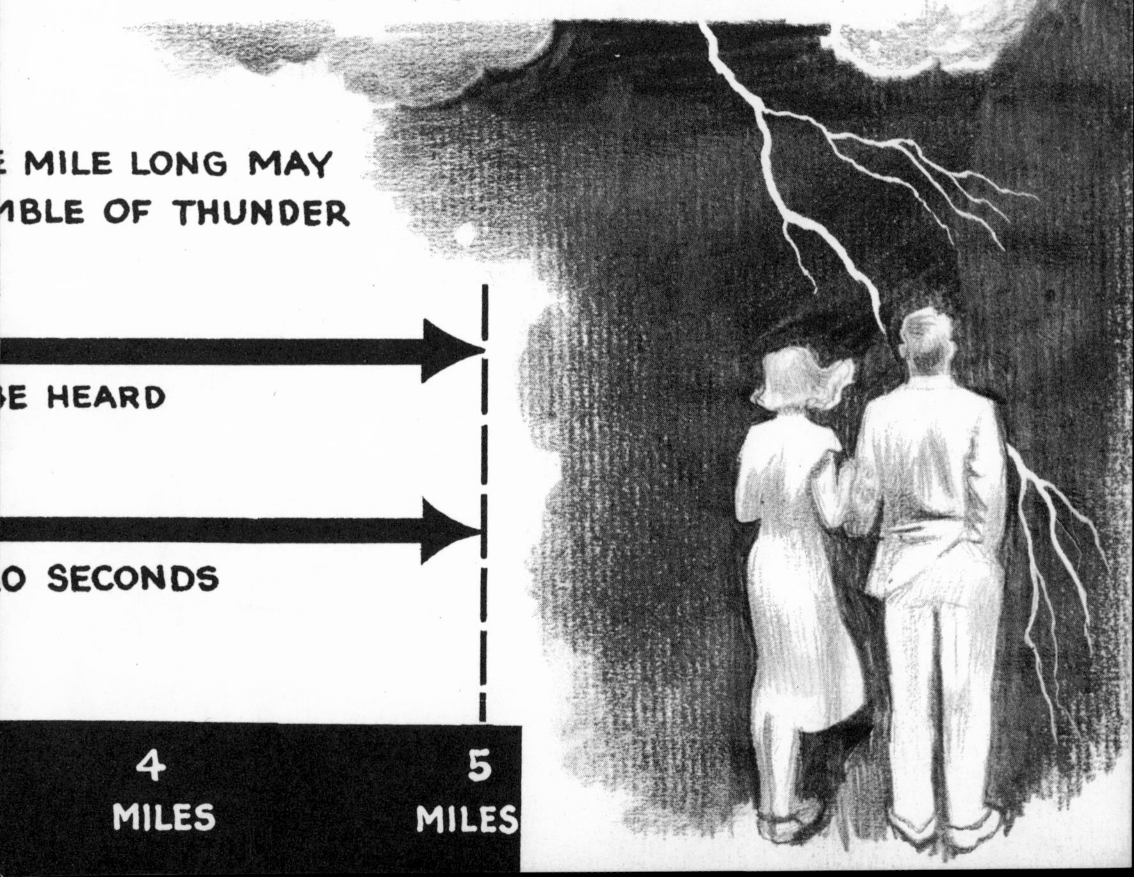

sap to steam so rapidly that an explosion occurs. The wood and bark are splintered and sometimes the entire tree is split to bits. Steam explosions like those in a tree may occur when lightning strikes any moist object, like a rain-soaked chimney or the mast of a ship.

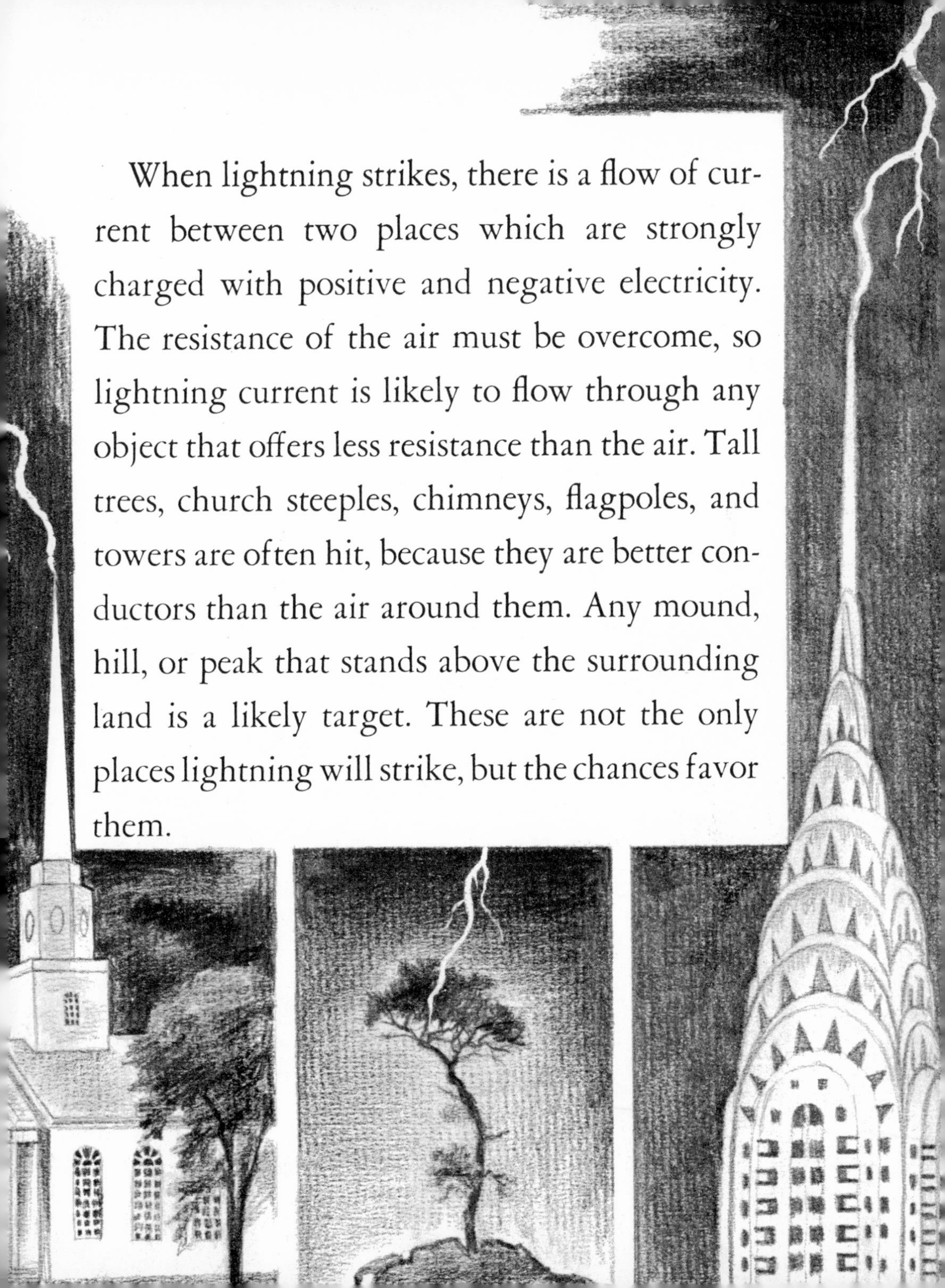

When lightning strikes, there is a flow of current between two places which are strongly charged with positive and negative electricity. The resistance of the air must be overcome, so lightning current is likely to flow through any object that offers less resistance than the air. Tall trees, church steeples, chimneys, flagpoles, and towers are often hit, because they are better conductors than the air around them. Any mound, hill, or peak that stands above the surrounding land is a likely target. These are not the only places lightning will strike, but the chances favor them.

The fact that lightning follows a good conductor suggests a fine way to protect ourselves from its danger. If one could build a large cage of heavy copper or iron bars, it would be the safest place during a thunderstorm. Lightning striking the cage would flow through the bars and would never harm the people inside. Such cages actually exist, though built for other reasons. A modern skyscraper is one of them. Its

EMPIRE STATE BUILDING
UNDER CONSTRUCTION AND FINISHED

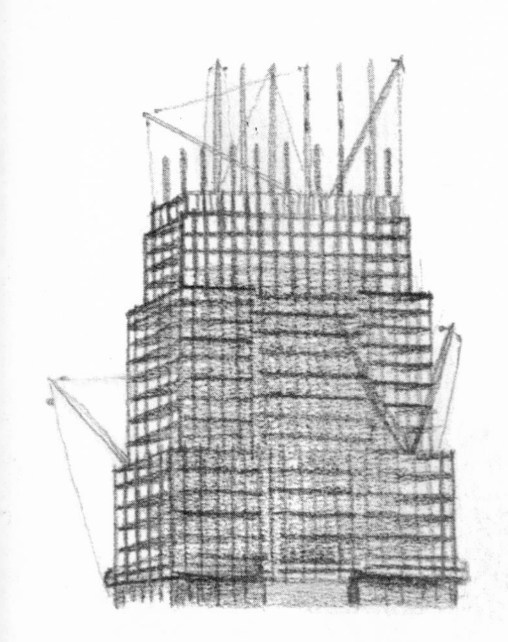

steel framework is a cage that protects everyone in the building. Lightning from most nearby storms strikes the Empire State Building in New York without doing any harm. Large steel bridges, steel ships, and huge gas tanks produce the same effect. A modern all-steel automobile is a lightning cage on wheels.

Most of the time it is not possible to have complete cage protection against lightning. Lightning rods are often used instead. A lightning rod is a rod of copper attached to the highest part of a building and connected to the ground by a copper cable. Benjamin Franklin and others had the idea for this kind of protection about 1750. Soon after, Franklin experimented with his silken kite and proved that lightning really is a form of electricity. A single

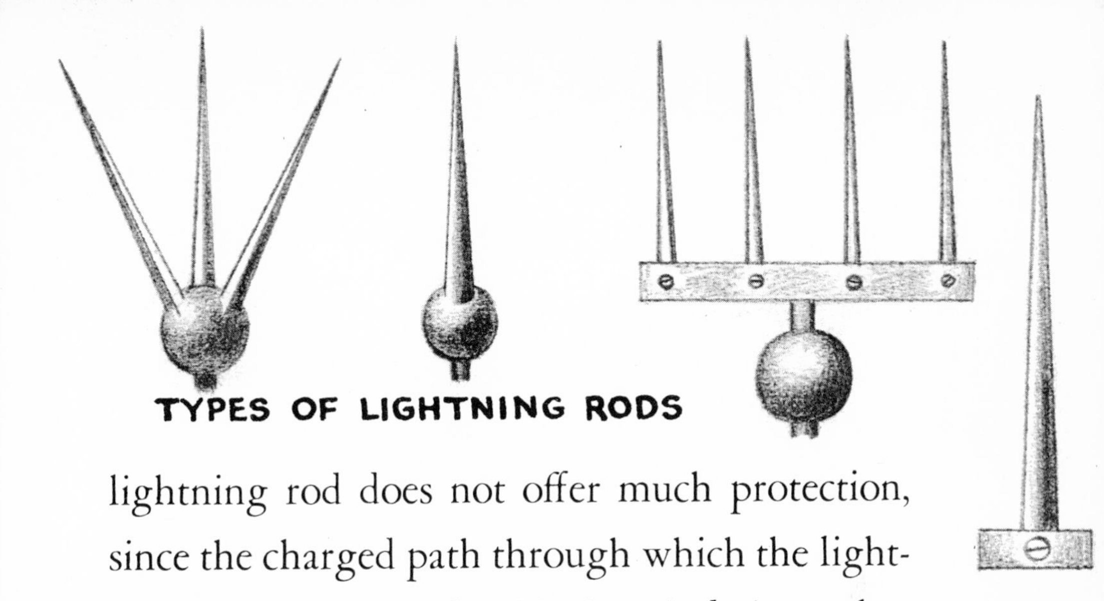

lightning rod does not offer much protection, since the charged path through which the lightning moves may shift with the wind. A number of lightning rods are usually set up in a system that gives protection to an entire building.

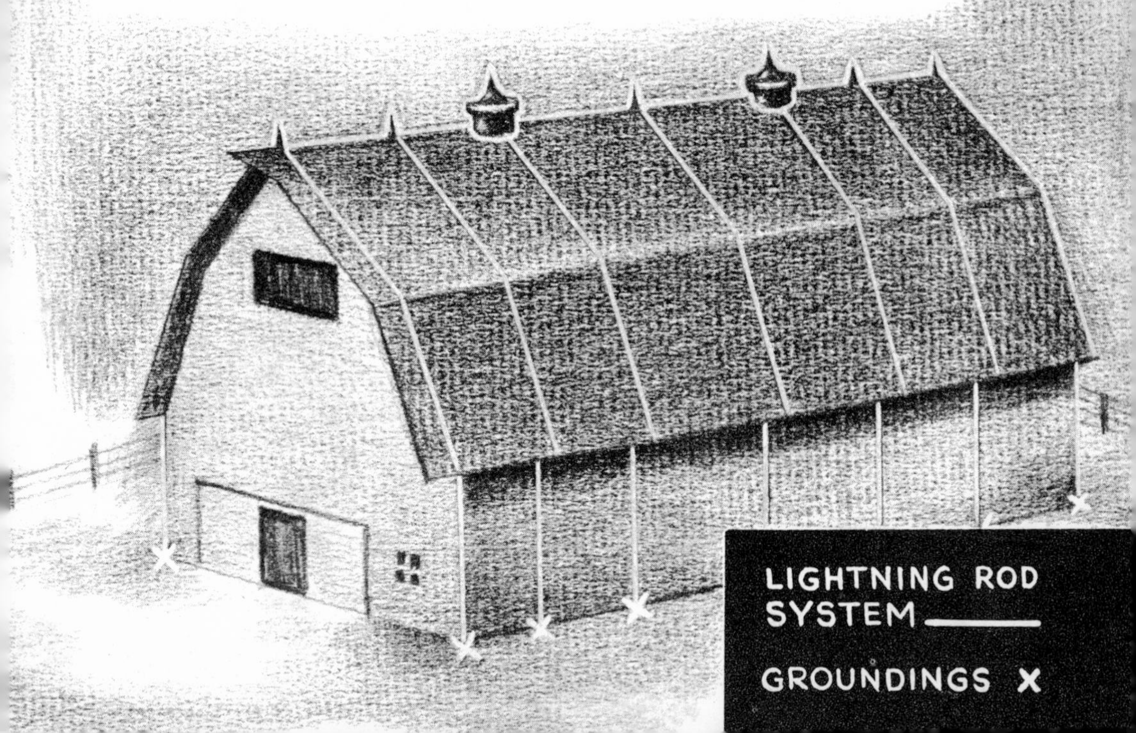

When lightning strikes buildings, it often starts fires. Many farm buildings are destroyed in this way. Each year lightning causes over 7,000 forest fires. Tall power lines, swinging high over the country, are constantly struck. The damage may leave a whole city in darkness and without

power. Ways have recently been found to let the lightning leap from the power lines down the tower and into the ground, thus cutting down its damage. Large machines making "artificial

lightning" have been set up in laboratories in order to study lightning and how to prevent damage to power lines. One machine makes a cur-

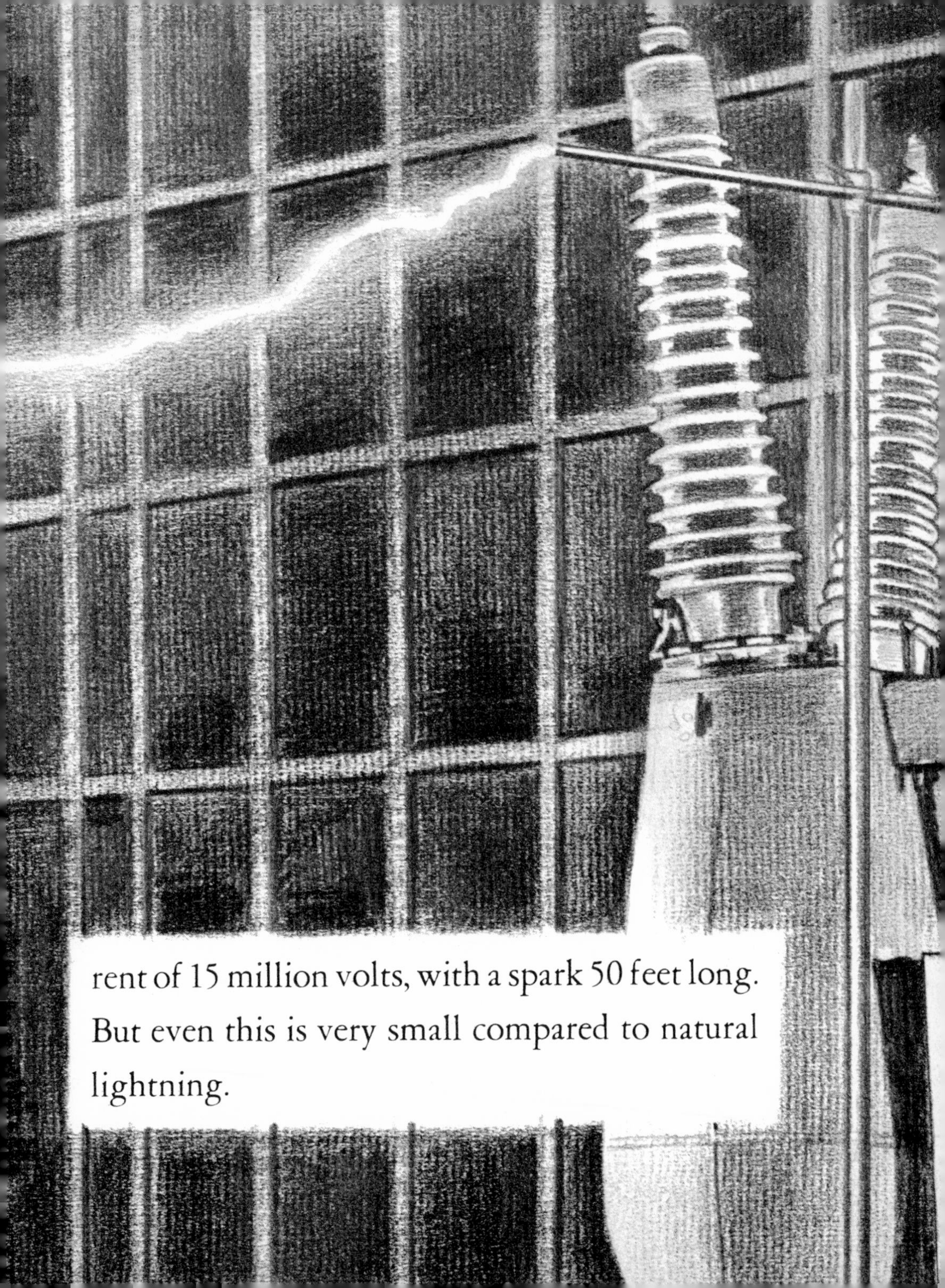

rent of 15 million volts, with a spark 50 feet long. But even this is very small compared to natural lightning.

Lightning has a useful side that few people know about. The tremendous energy of each lightning flash causes some of the nitrogen and oxygen in the air to combine. Nitrogen is a gas that makes up four fifths of the air. Plants need it in order to grow. It is an important part of meat and other foods. But the nitrogen in the air is useless. It is only of use to plants and to us when it has joined with oxygen or some other chemical, and lightning helps it to do just that. The newly made nitrogen chemicals are brought down to the ground with rain and are absorbed by the soil. About four pounds of nitrogen are added to an acre of land each year. While this is a small amount, the natural, lightning-made fertilizer does have some value.

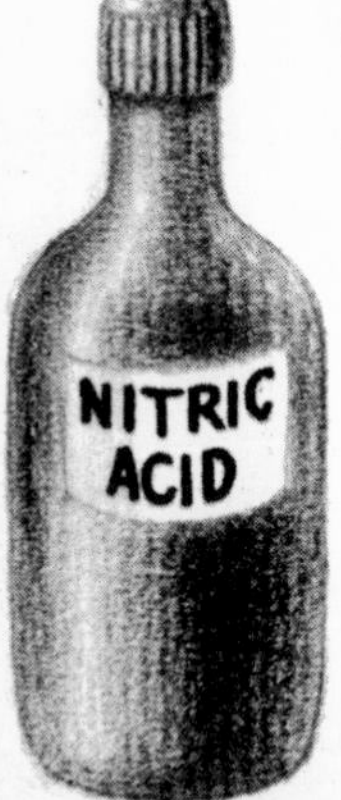

100 TO 500 MILLION TONS
ARE MADE BY LIGHTNING EACH YEAR

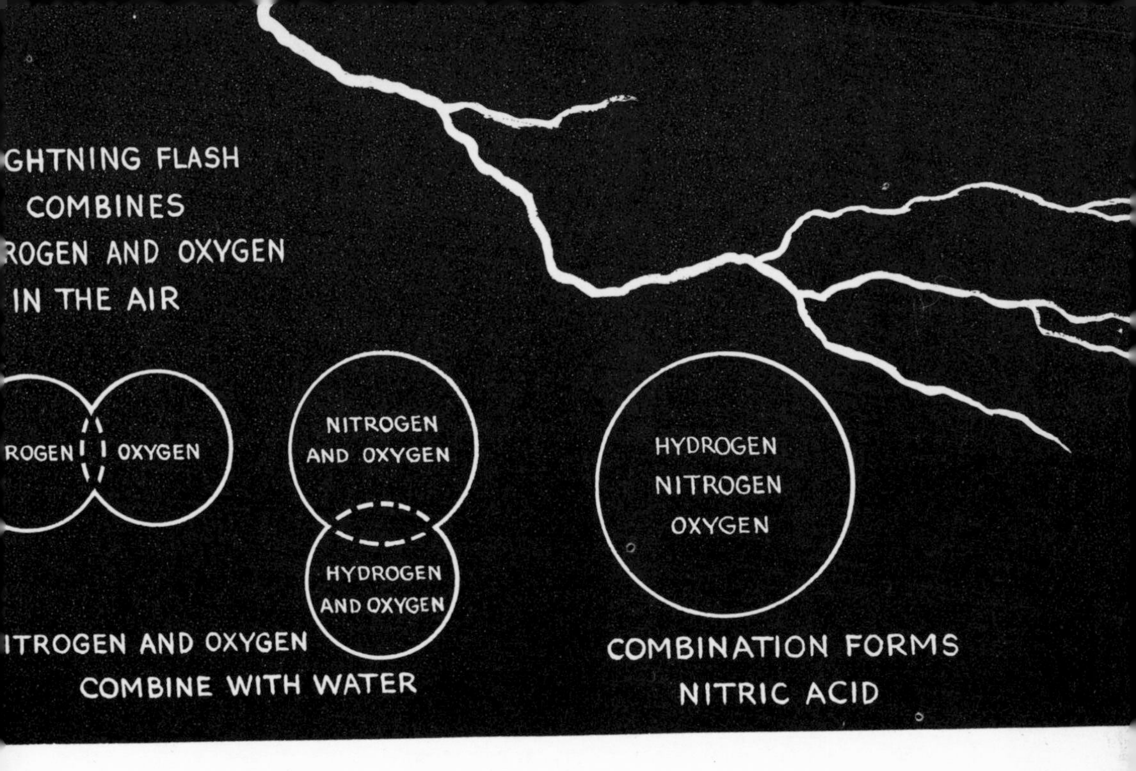

Lightning also causes the oxygen in the air to change from its usual form to a special active form known as ozone. Oxygen has no odor. Ozone has. The strong sulphur-like smell that people notice when lightning has struck nearby is partly ozone. Layers of ozone high in the air help protect the earth from the ultraviolet part of the sunlight, the part that causes sunburn.

OZONE LAYERS

15 MILES

10 MILES

MT. EVEREST
5½ MILES

5 MILES

Lightning may have freak effects. It causes a tube of copper to partly melt and collapse. It may fuse metal parts together. Lightning hitting a golf course has left a spreading pattern of scorched grass behind. Striking a beach, the

lightning may fuse the sand into a glassy rod of silica rock. Lightning may jump from one conductor to another, and may travel along a wire fence before it leaps to the ground. There is no end to the stories of freak lightning strokes.

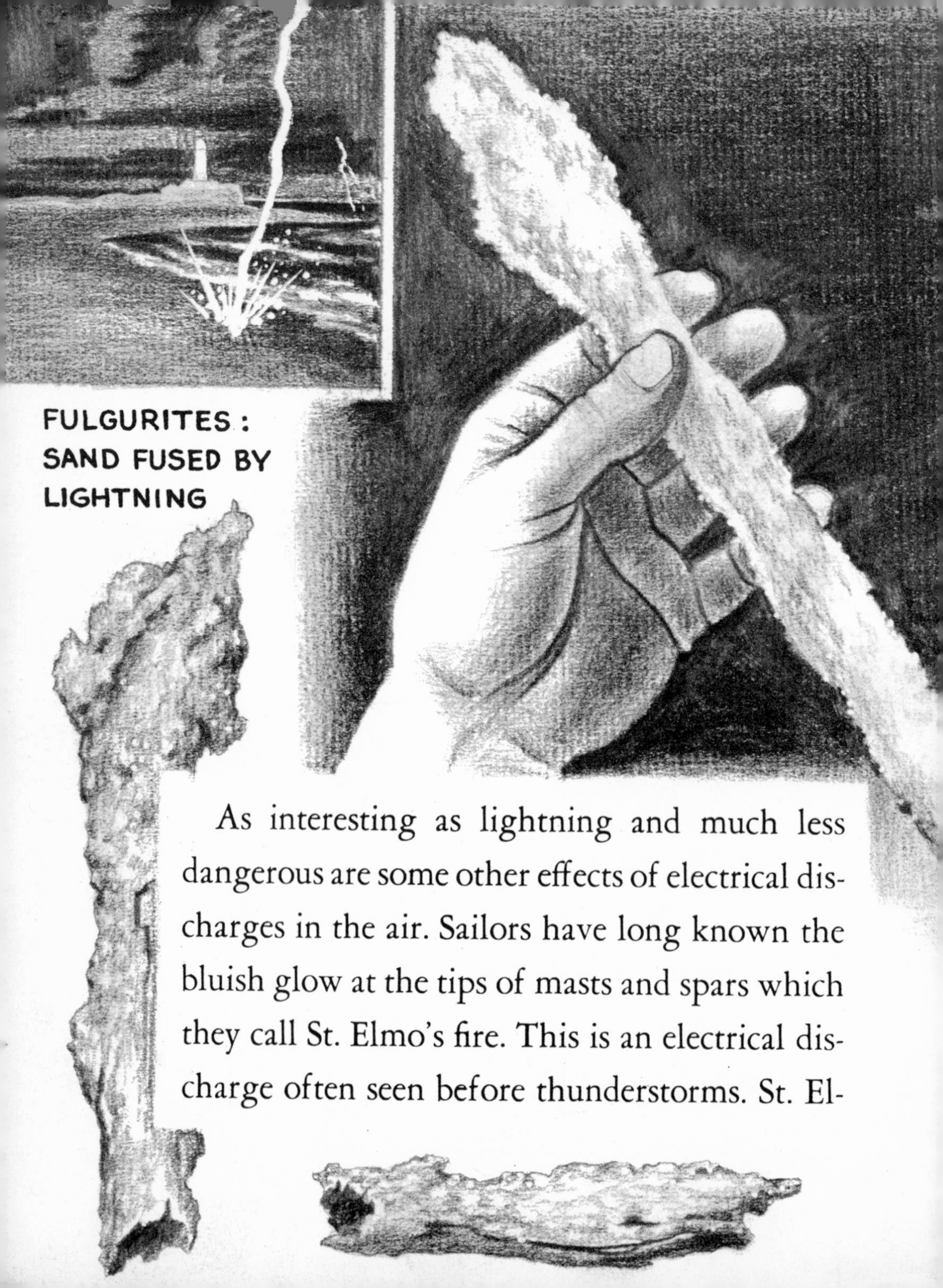

As interesting as lightning and much less dangerous are some other effects of electrical discharges in the air. Sailors have long known the bluish glow at the tips of masts and spars which they call St. Elmo's fire. This is an electrical discharge often seen before thunderstorms. St. El-

mo's fire can also be seen on the tips of airplane wings when the plane is flying near thunder-storms.

As far as we know, lightning cannot be controlled, and as long as our earth remains there will be thunderstorms. We have found several ways to limit the damage that lightning can do. Because we understand more about lightning and thunder, we have less reason to fear them. Nowadays most people take lightning for what it really is–the most unusual and most exciting part of all our weather.

DATE DUE	BORROWER'S NAME	ROOM NUMBER
May 2	Carmen	
May 9	Dawn	
" 16	Patty	
6/5/67	Karen	

DON'T WORK IN
AN OPEN FIELD
DON'T
SWIM
DON'T
DON'T STAY UNDER
A LONE TREE
DON'T STAY NEAR
A WIRE FENCE
DON'T STAY ON A
HIGH, EXPOSED PL